KEEPING WELL
A GUIDE TO HEALTH IN RETIREMENT

Anne Roberts is a doctor specializing in the care of the elderly. During her long experience she has become an acknowledged expert whose advice and knowledge are sought by charities and other bodies. Her main current interest is in teaching those who care for old people, such as wardens of sheltered housing, staff of old people's homes, nurses and home helps. She is the author of *A Warden's Guide to Health Care in Sheltered Housing* published by Age Concern, and wrote the health section in *The Time of Your Life* for Help the Aged. She co-wrote the *New Faber Anatomical Atlas* and writes regularly for *Nursing Times*. She is on the Board of Management of the Anchor Housing Association which specializes in sheltered housing for the elderly and sits on numerous working parties concerned with housing and health care for retired people.

She lives in south London with her husband, a child psychiatrist, and their two children.

Some other Faber health titles

THE FERTILITY AND CONTRACEPTION BOOK *Julia Mosse and Josephine Heaton*
ALZHEIMER'S DISEASE: THE LONG BEREAVEMENT *Elizabeth Forsythe*
MULTIPLE SCLEROSIS: EXPLORING SICKNESS AND HEALTH *Elizabeth Forsythe*
SLEEP AND DREAMING *Jacob Empson*
DRUG USE AND ABUSE *James Willis*
FOOD FACTS AND FIGURES *Jill Davies and John Dickerson*
UNDERSTANDING YOUR CHILD *Richard Woolfson*
EVERYWOMAN: A GYNAECOLOGICAL GUIDE FOR LIFE Fifth Edition *Derek Llewellyn-Jones*
FABER POCKET-MEDICAL DICTIONARY *Elizabeth Forsythe*
CERVICAL CANCER *Judith Harvey, Sue Mack and Julian Woolfson*
SAFER SEX *Peter Gordon and Louise Mitchell*
ANOREXIA NERVOSA: THE BROKEN CIRCLE *Ann Erichsen*
AGORAPHOBIA *Ruth Hurst Voce*
YOUR CHILD'S HEALTH *Ivan Blumenthal*
SICKLE CELL DISEASE *Ian Franklin*
AQUAROBICS *Glenda Baum*

Keeping Well

A Guide to Health in Retirement

ANNE ROBERTS, MB, BS, MRCP

faber and faber
LONDON·BOSTON

First published 1991
by Faber and Faber Limited
3 Queen Square London WC1N 3AU

Photoset by Wilmaset, Birkenhead, Wirral
Printed in Great Britain by
Clays Ltd, St Ives Plc

Anne Roberts is hereby identified as author of this work
in accordance with Section 77 of the Copyright, Design
and Patents Act 1988.

A CIP record for this book is available from the British Library

ISBN 0-571-15494-8

For my parents
Eddie and Monica Roberts
with love

Contents

Introduction

If you are a pensioner now, you will have had an eventful life. You will have come through at least one World War, with the dangers of military service, the risks and weariness of the Blitz, worry over loved ones far away and the tedium of 'making do'. You may remember the horrors of an earlier war: the empty places at family gatherings and the filling of war memorials with name after name. You can remember other hard times – the Depression of the thirties and the rigours of post-war austerity in the forties and early fifties. When people got ill in your young days, there was little the doctor could do to help, even if you could afford to pay him. You can recall babies, children and young adults dying of diseases like diphtheria, measles or tuberculosis, which can be prevented or treated now. It took a robust generation to come through, using all you had of intelligence, common sense and the capacity to work hard and adapt to changing circumstances. A tough lot, you elderly people; the others have not survived to tell the tale.

The physical and, even more so, the mental strengths of older people are often ignored by well-meaning givers of advice. You may have resented being 'talked down to' in this way, and have understandably ignored what you have been told.

This book is different; it assumes you must have common sense and practical ability, or you would be neither here to read it nor interested in improving your skills further. What is more, it emphasizes self-help and patient-involvement. Most people are happier when they feel in charge of their own destiny, and there is evidence that this attitude promotes mental health too. The slavish following of 'doctor's orders' is now out of date. Instead, intelligent patients of whatever age like to know what is happening to them when they are ill and what sorts of treatment are available. They are then able to hold their own in discussion with doctors and other health care professionals and to make their own wishes understood. If this is how you like to cope with your own health problems, then this is the book for you.

The book has four main chapters. Chapter 1 is about lifestyle and describes ways in which an elderly person can stay healthy enough to enjoy his or her independence. Chapter 2 gives accounts of the commoner illnesses of later life, what the doctor can do to help and how the sufferers can help themselves. Chapter 3 contains general information about medicines and how to get the most from them, followed by further details of the most commonly used types. Chapter 4 describes sources of help. It is followed by a list of useful addresses of helpful organizations and a book list containing suggestions for further reading.

Some parts of the book – the healthy living chapter, for instance – can comfortably be read through. Others, such as the medicines chapter, are more likely to be referred to from time to time.

To find your way about the book, use the index on pages 175–83, as different aspects of a subject will be covered in different chapters. For example, basic information about the nature of Parkinson's Disease will be found in Chapter 2, and details of its drug treatment in Chapter 3. Suggestions for getting help to cope with the difficulties arising from it are in Chapter 4, while the address and telephone number of the Parkinson's Disease Society are in the Useful Addresses section.

I

Staying Healthy in Later Life

The major life-change of retirement is often thrust on employees, whether or not they are ready for it. Self-employed people may have more choice: provided the work is available, they can continue to do it for as long as they like. Eventually most people choose to step down their work commitments, if not to retire completely.

A newly retired person finds both losses and gains in his or her changed life. On the one hand, income may fall, and the loss of social contacts with workmates may lead to loneliness unless and until new friends are found. Some people feel a great loss of status and job satisfaction on leaving work, although this is not invariable. On the other hand, it may be a joy to have more time for family, friends and leisure interests.

To feel fulfilled at this time of life, most people need to feel useful to someone else. It also helps to retain some sort of personal discipline and structure to the day – to get up at a reasonable time, eat proper meals and take care of personal appearance, for instance. Another important ingredient of a happy and active retirement is good health, and the lifestyle described in this chapter helps to ensure this. Topics covered include diet and eating habits, use of alcohol, smoking, taking exercise, keeping safe, and sex and loving. More nebulous but equally important subjects – stress, worry and mental health – follow, and the chapter ends with a discussion of body maintenance and when to call the doctor.

Food

People's eating habits often change when they retire. Some people gain weight once they have ready access to food stores and home cooking. Others eat less well, perhaps because they lack the skills to shop for and cook hot main meals like the ones formerly provided in the canteen at work. A little 'thought for food' around this time of life is often useful, as good eating helps maintain health and fitness. This section concentrates on the aspects of nutrition that matter most to older people.

What is a good diet?

This should contain *enough energy* (usually expressed in calories) to keep the body at its ideal weight, neither too fat nor too thin. It should also contain *enough nutrients*. A varied diet ensures this; a person in normal health who eats some foods from each of the following groups daily does not need supplements of vitamins or minerals:

- *meat and its alternatives*, e.g. poultry, offal, fish, eggs, nuts, pulses (peas, beans and lentils).
- *starchy foods* – preferably unrefined – e.g. wholemeal bread, potatoes, wholegrain cereals, brown rice and pasta. Refined starches found in cakes and biscuits contain energy as calories but less fibre and nutrients.
- *dairy foods* – milk, cheese and yoghurt.
- *fruit and vegetables*.

Changes in body composition and weight with age

Although the weight of a healthy person's body should stay steady, its composition will change. As the years pass, lean body mass, made up of bone, muscle and body organs, falls. This change partly accounts for the osteoporosis (see page 74), decline in athletic performance and loss of reserve capacity of body systems which occur with increasing age. The loss of mass is made good by putting on fat, and this causes changes in the shape of the body; while women tend to lay down fat around the midriff and hips, men store it within the torso, sometimes forming an overhanging paunch.

Most of the energy burnt by sedentary people is accounted for by the basal metabolic rate (BMR). This is a measure of the energy used by the body at rest, rather like the petrol consumption of a car standing still with the engine running. The BMR declines progressively with age, by 5 per cent for each decade from 40–60 years old and by 10 per cent for each decade thereafter. Therefore, to avoid progressive weight-gain from mid-life onwards, either energy expenditure must be increased or calorie intake reduced. On the whole, it is best to take at least some exercise, as too stringent cutbacks in food volume may imperil the supply of nutrients.

Being overweight
People of normal weight in old age are healthier than their fatter counterparts. They run less risk of illnesses like diabetes, stroke, heart disease or gallstones, put less strain on their heart, lungs and joints and are less likely to have accidents.

An honest look in a full-length mirror may be enough to convince you that you need to lose weight, or you may prefer to consult height/weight tables. You may want to discuss weight loss with your doctor if you have health worries, if you have more than a stone or so to lose, or if you have tried to lose weight without succeeding.

Principles of weight loss
- You only lose weight when your body burns more energy than is fed into it.
- Aim to eat less – about half to two-thirds of your previous intake. Main cut-backs should be in 'empty calories', the foods that provide fuel but few nutrients, such as sugars, refined starches and alcohol. Be sparing with fats. Instead, eat more fruit, vegetables and unrefined starches; for instance, whole-

meal bread and jacket potatoes are filling and suitable if fatty or sugary spreads and toppings are avoided. Do not waste money on special diet foods.

- Get support from family and friends; there may also be help for dieters at their health centre or doctor's surgery.
- Find your weak spots and avoid temptation. It may help to keep away from food between meals; keep low-calorie snacks such as apples, carrots and celery handy; avoid buying sweets or cakes; shop with a pre-written list, and never when hungry; build in rewards for effort – obviously not food treats.
- Permanent weight-loss is a slow process; 2–4 lb loss in the first week and 1–2 lb per week thereafter would be grounds for satisfaction.
- A long-term healthy eating pattern is necessary to maintain ideal weight. Crash diets do not give long-term benefit.

Being underweight
Small fluctuations in weight are common: most of us expect to put on a few pounds over Christmas or our holiday, or to lose a little if we have 'flu or go through an anxious time. In normal circumstances the situation soon rights itself. An unexplained weight loss, whether sudden or gradual, is not normal. In frailer, older pensioners especially, it can be the sign of an illness such as cancer, thyroid disease, an infection, cardiac failure, depression, dementia or the effects of some medicines. Prompt medical attention gives the best chance of a good outcome. Once the cause is found, correction is sometimes easy, and the old person can start to enjoy life again.

Although we need fewer calories as the years advance, we need the same amount of nutrients. These therefore have to be taken in a smaller volume of food, and there is less capacity to be spared for empty calories contained in sweets, cakes, biscuits and alcohol. Unfortunately, high-nutrient foods tend to require more preparation than less nourishing snacks such as biscuits and tea, and people who are frail, disabled or convalescent may lack the motivation, ability and skills to feed themselves properly. If you know someone in this situation, you may like to refer to the suggestions on 'Help with meals' in Chapter 4 (pages 156–7).

Cooking for older people
Cooking for an older person with a capricious appetite can be frustrating. Of course, it helps to consult their likes and dislikes as far as possible, and to serve small portions presented attractively and in forms that are easy to eat. A small amount of a favourite alcoholic drink before a meal may stimulate appetite. If things remain difficult, consult the doctor, nurse or dietitian for further advice. A final word – the preparation and eating of food are highly symbolic activities, with food signifying love in many people's deepest consciousness. It is important to remember that rejection of a lovingly prepared meal is not necessarily intended as a rejection of the preparer; it may simply mean that the recipient is not hungry.

Getting enough fibre
Fibre, sometimes called roughage, helps to prevent constipation and bowel conditions such as diverticular disease and piles. Fruit, vegetables and the unrefined starchy foods are good sources, as are the pulses, which also contain some protein.

Many of us need more fibre, but it is wise to increase intake gradually and to take ample fluids to avoid digestive upset.

Taking enough fluids
The sense of thirst dulls with age, so an older person can unknowingly become dehydrated. This is dangerous, jeopardizing kidney and brain function and making blood-flow to vital organs sluggish. 3–5 pints of liquid per day are needed to compensate for fluid lost from the body; losses increase during hot weather and in someone with a feverish illness, a weeping ulcer or diarrhoea. Someone who is drinking enough should pass pale-coloured urine, except for first thing in the morning. Though small amounts of alcoholic drinks are a harmless pleasure it is

worth remembering that because they increase urine-flow, their net effect is fluid *loss*.

It is obviously sensible to organize fluid intake so that the need to visit the lavatory comes at a convenient time. However, it is risky to cut back on the twenty-four-hour total; if fluids are being restricted because of the fear of incontinence, it is sensible to seek medical help.

The importance of fruit and vegetables

These provide Vitamin C which promotes healing, keeps blood vessels healthy and helps the body to absorb some other nutrients, such as iron. Fruit and vegetables also contain folate to help prevent anaemia, and are good sources of fibre.

The body cannot store Vitamin C for long, so foods containing it are best taken daily. It is fragile and easily destroyed by cooking, so raw foods are more reliable sources. An orange a day or the equivalent in fruit juice fills the need in winter; in summer, strawberries or other fresh fruit may work out cheaper per serving. Blackcurrant or rosehip syrup may be preferred by people who find citrus and other fruits too sharp.

Restricting fat

Fats such as butter and margarine, the fat on meat or beneath chicken skin, in made-up foods like sausages and pies and in whole milk and full-fat dairy produce contain many calories; all should be eaten sparingly if you are watching your weight. Instead, choose low-fat cheeses and spreads, and skimmed or semi-skimmed milk. Trimming meat of visible fat, discarding chicken skin and grilling rather than frying food all help to keep fat intake low.

Saturated fats of animal origin may be linked with heart disease. This connection becomes weaker in later life, as the most vulnerable people do not survive middle age. If you have recently retired, or are planning to do so in the near future, it is probably sensible to reduce your total fat intake as described above and to substitute polyunsaturates such as sunflower oil and margarine for saturated fats in the remainder. If you are over seventy-five, the type of fat you take is probably less important to your health, but you would still be well advised to reduce your total fat intake if you are overweight.

It is worth remembering that we all need *some* fat in our diet; while many of us would benefit from cutting down on fats, a few would not: these include very frail elderly people with tiny appetites who need food rich in calories to give sufficient energy in a small volume.

Fractures – eating to avoid them

Women's bones weaken faster than men's do as time passes, because of the after-effects of the menopause. Hormone replacement therapy (HRT) is the most effective way for women to keep their bones strong. Adequate calcium, which stiffens the bones, and Vitamin D, needed for calcium metabolism, help too. Half a pint of milk a day, skimmed or semi-skimmed if preferred, and half a pound of cheese per week or its equivalent in other dairy produce gives enough calcium. Though some Vitamin D can be made in the skin on exposure to sunlight during the summer months, a dietary boost is often needed, especially in winter. Fit people in normal health should take a weekly portion of oily fish, such as herring, mackerel, pilchards, sardines, tuna or tinned salmon. Someone who is housebound or who has difficulties with absorbing their food may need a Vit D supplement from the doctor.

Enjoying your food

Eating should be fun. It is worth remembering that no *one* food is essential for health; attractive and healthy substitutes can almost always be found for an unrelished item. For instance, wholemeal bread is not compulsory; if you prefer white, eat it and get extra fibre elsewhere. The regular healthy eating pattern is what matters; the occasional 'treat' – a cream cake, fried breakfast or chocolate sundae – will not affect your health and may make it easier to eat sensibly the rest of the time.

Those who live alone and cook just for themselves may find it more difficult to get pleasure from preparing and eating meals, despite realizing the importance of a good diet. To maintain interest in eating, it helps to use recipes that avoid waste and are not too difficult or lengthy. Some sources of these are mentioned in the book list. Newly retired people who have rarely had to cook for themselves may find cookery classes useful and stimulating. Variety in the diet is important for health reasons, and something different – an unusual fruit or variety of cheese, perhaps – also helps to prevent boredom. Many solitary eaters think it important to set the table properly when eating alone – though a tray in front of the TV from time to time will not lead to an irreversible decline in standards.

Readers who would like to know more about nutrition or who would like suggestions to extend their cooking skills should refer to the book list on pages 171–4.

Enjoying alcohol in later life

Most people who drink alcohol enjoy it sensibly whatever their age. A few suffer ill-effects, and older people, especially women, become more vulnerable to these. This is because bodily changes with age affect tolerance even in lifelong drinkers. Risks of over-indulgence include mental confusion, worsening of a tendency to fall or to be incontinent of urine, malnourishment and loneliness if the heavy drinker becomes unpleasant company.

The risks of light drinking are very small. A recommended maximum safe level is:

4–6 units 2–3 times per week for an older man
   (i.e. 8–18 units per week)
2–3 units 2–3 times per week for an older woman
   (i.e. 4–9 units per week)

A unit is:
a single measure of spirits, or
½ pint normal strength beer, or

1 glass wine, or
1 small glass sherry, port or vermouth.

Unmeasured drinks poured at home, half pints of extra-strength beers and large glasses such as sherry schooners usually contain several units. People with health problems affecting their balance or who take certain medicines may be harmed by even smaller amounts of alcohol than these recommendations.

The alcohol 'ration' can be spaced through the week however the drinker likes, though alcohol-free days (AFDs) are advisable. People who drink daily while keeping within the recommended weekly total only increase their risk level slightly.

When watching your drinking, it helps to find a soft non-alcoholic drink you enjoy. This can be drunk on AFDs or used to space alcoholic drinks at parties. Hosts and hostesses may want to serve a range of soft drinks for health-conscious drinkers and for drivers.

If you need to cut down a little, it can help to keep a diary of when, where and with whom you drink, so temptation can be avoided. Information of this sort can help you keep control of this aspect of your life as you do of others.

If you are worried about your drinking, help is available. Details of agencies countrywide are available from Alcohol Concern, and lists of services in London and the Home Counties from the Greater London Alcohol Advisory Service (see page 169). Alternatively your health centre, CAB or Community Health Council may be able to help – or look under 'Alcohol' in the telephone book. If you fear your drinking could be affecting your health, it is wise to consult your doctor.

Sense about smoking

Many older smokers took up the habit before it was known to be harmful to health. Some started during World War II when they were preoccupied with immediate danger and the long-term consequences seemed of academic interest only. Now we know that smoking kills 100,000 people a year in the UK, each smoker dying on average ten years before his or her time. Smoking causes lung cancer, bronchitis and emphysema, heart and blood vessel diseases including heart attacks and strokes, worsens peptic ulcers and makes an anaesthetic for an operation more risky. It also worsens chest infections, breathlessness and cough from whatever cause and raises blood pressure.

You may feel that after smoking for, say, forty years, it is too late to give up, but research shows this to be wrong. Health risks, for example from heart disease, start to decline from the day the last cigarette is smoked, and after ten years' abstinence the risk of lung cancer is almost as low as in a non-smoker.

The secret of giving up smoking is to want to; there are about eight million ex-smokers in the UK who have already done so. Advice may help; you may want to get in touch with ASH (see page 167), read the publication mentioned in the book list, or find out whether there are leaflets at your doctor's surgery or a support group in your area. Encouragement from family and friends is invaluable, especially if they are non-smokers. As with alcohol, it may help you to record the circumstances in which you are most likely to smoke, so as to avoid danger times. If you smoke more under stress, it may help to think seriously about other ways of handling anxiety. Some people find sucking strong-flavoured sweets or dummy cigarettes useful. Others are helped by using nicotine-containing chewing gum (Nicorette), obtained on private prescription from their doctor. Thinking of new uses for the money saved – often several hundred pounds a year – can also stiffen willpower.

Many people find withdrawal easier than they expected; even those who have difficulties usually find the worst is over in a month. Weight gain can follow, but the excess is usually lost without much difficulty; even if retained, the extra weight affects your health less than continued smoking. Don't despair if you lapse during the first attempt; many people stop successfully after several false starts. It may help your perseverance to remember that giving up cigarettes is the most effective self-help step to health in retirement – to your own health and that of others, such as grandchildren, who may be influenced by your example.

Taking exercise

Televised marathon races have shown us all that older people can be successful athletes. Modern research reveals that less drastic activity can improve health prospects in later life, some participants becoming fitter than they were in youth. Taken regularly, exercise boosts the efficiency of the heart and lungs, giving the stamina to meet extra stress from unaccustomed activity or sudden illness. Strengthened muscles protect the back from injury and reduce the risk of falls, while mobile joints in a supple body ensure personal independence. Bones are strengthened by activity, and the circulation of blood to heart and limbs is improved, helping to prevent heart attacks and other circulation disorders.

How to go about exercising

People who already participate in sports are well advised to continue doing so as they get older, at a sensible pace; it is unwise to try to compete with younger players or with one's own past records.

Retirement can provide new opportunities to increase fitness after a hectic but sedentary working life. However, someone out of training who suddenly embarks on a strenuous activity like jogging or squash in retirement is likely to injure himself. More suitable activities include swimming, cycling where the roads are safe to do so, exercise classes, dancing or yoga. Brisk walking is a cheap and convenient form of exercise that can usually be built in to any day's routine. From a slow start, a good aim is to build up to covering a mile in twenty minutes, once or twice a day. Whatever the type of exercise you choose, it is important to find one you enjoy enough to persevere with, as health benefits cease once the activity is stopped.

Although outdoor exercise is pleasant, it may be sensible to plan an alternative for when the weather is bad. Books and tapes (audio and video) are available to help with exercising at home, but it takes great motivation to do this regularly. Joining a class is a more reliable way of making oneself stay active, and the least athletic 'non-joiner' may be surprised to discover how much he or she enjoys exercise sessions in cheerful company.

The following points are worth noting:

• If you suffer from high blood pressure or have chest, heart or joint problems, it makes sense to check with your doctor before starting an exercise programme, as some sorts of exercise may be more suitable for you than others.
• Always start an exercise session slowly and increase activity levels gradually, winding down at the end. Stop and rest if you become unduly short of breath or develop chest pains or palpitations. Don't force a painful joint; no movement should hurt at the time, though a little stiffness in newly active muscles is to be expected the next day.

It is wise to take it easy when you or prevailing conditions are not at their best. Do not risk a fall when ice or wet leaves make the going treacherous, and avoid strenuous exercise when you are unwell, for instance with a cold. If you enjoy attending a Keep Fit class but have joint, balance or sight difficulties, it makes sense to participate in the safe activities and sit out any exercises you find difficult or painful.

To find out more about opportunities in your area, you could get in touch with Extend or the Keep Fit Association (see pages 168 and 169). Your local public library will have details of leisure activities and adult education classes.

Even very frail elderly people benefit from keeping active, as this helps them to continue to look after themselves despite, perhaps, some degree of disability. It is a useful exercise to stretch all the joints daily through their full range of movement, especially the shoulders, as suppleness here makes washing the face and combing the hair possible. A word of warning – a painful joint should not be forced into mobility in the mistaken belief that it will otherwise become fixed; no exercise should hurt at the time it is performed. Someone who is over eighty and disabled herself, Laura Mitchell, has written a useful book on this subject (see book list).

Keeping safe

You have reached your present age and position by adapting to changing circumstances and by carefully balancing risk-taking and safe behaviour. This same approach will help you to enjoy an active and independent retirement, as long as you allow for the ageing changes in your body. Many people find that with increasing age their vision and hearing become less sharp and they are slower on their feet. If they are honest about these difficulties, they can seek appropriate help and often improve their abilities. If they accept any remaining limitations they can then keep as independent as possible without running unnecessary risks. Of course, *some* risk-taking is necessary if life is to be active and enjoyable at any age. On the whole, old people suffer more from the results of underactivity than from those of accidents; you may want to bear this in mind if you are caring for older, frailer friends or relatives. Nevertheless, recklessness may threaten independence if, for instance, an older person finds it difficult to get back on their feet after breaking a hip.

On the road

Walking
Pedestrian crossings are the safest place to cross roads; in few countries outside the UK is it legal to cross urban roads wherever one likes, and it is certainly dangerous here.

   Where there is no pavement, choose the side of the road on which you will face oncoming traffic as you walk. A particularly hazardous place to cross the road is within the hundred yards or so either side of a crossing, as the driver's attention is focussed either ahead or behind. Street lighting is often poor, and as drivers know, dark-clad pedestrians may be almost invisible after dusk.

If you are out after dark it makes sense to wear some light clothing or even a Day-Glo band.

Cycling

Cycling is excellent exercise and a pollution-free way of getting about. Sadly, it is now necessary for any cyclist, particularly an older one, to examine local conditions carefully, as in some places heavy traffic now makes it too dangerous to ride a bike.

All cyclists are well advised to wear reflective clothing and to check their bike brakes and also their lights – working ones seem to be the exception rather than the rule. Looking on the blackest side, cyclists' most serious injuries involve their heads; you may want to consider buying a good cycling helmet.

Driving

As you will know, the standard full driving licence is valid until the holder's seventieth birthday. Although there is no legal maximum age, drivers past this milestone have to renew their licence every three years, declaring that their health continues good and that they have no disability interfering with their driving safety. If you are concerned that your health or any medication you take may be affecting your driving, you would be well advised to consult your doctor. Some people also get an unbiased opinion of their abilities by arranging for an hour or two with a driving instructor.

Drivers are *obliged* to notify the Department of Transport in Swansea of certain changes in their health. Relevant disabilities include:

- Any possible cause of a sudden loss of consciousness at the wheel.
- Any illness that interferes with visual ability, whether visual acuity (seeing clearly), visual fields (seeing to either side) or dark adaptation.
- Mental abnormalities that interfere with judgement and reduce concentration.
- Severe deafness.

- Conditions interfering with dexterity and movement, if they affect the ability to handle a car's controls.

If the DVLC is unhappy about your reported health, you may be required to ask your own doctor to supply further information. If there is still doubt, you may need to be examined by a nominated doctor.

In general it is wise for older drivers to make things easy for themselves. For instance, without the time-constraints of a working life it will usually be possible to avoid travelling at night and during rush hours. Forward planning of routes, regular rests and realism about the distance to be travelled in a day also help to reduce the risk of tiredness and mishap. It goes without saying that no one of any age should ever drink and drive.

Averting the threat of crime

Despite media publicity, older people are less likely than younger ones to fall victim to 'personal' crimes such as mugging, which are usually dreaded more than crimes against property. Small risks can be reduced still further by taking sensible steps. While it is unfortunately easy to put off doing so during a busy working life, retirement is a good time to reconsider all your security precautions. You may want to visit your local police station to ask for advice or to make contact with the Crime Prevention Officer. In some areas he or she will visit your home free of charge to advise on improving your security, recommending reliable firms to fit locks and similar devices. The local police will also know if yours is a Neighbourhood Watch area. In many places retired people are the mainstay of these groups, and you may want to join.

Home security

Eighty per cent of 'break-ins' are no such thing: an amateur thief simply enters by an open door or window. If instead he finds difficulties in his way, he will often move on to an easier property rather than chance attracting attention by breaking glass. Risks can be reduced by taking sensible steps, and suggestions for further precautions are included here as an aid to peace of mind. It makes sense to fit good security deadlocks to doors, with bolts at top and bottom. Window locks are also important, and the glass slats of louvres should be glued in place, or they can be easily removed to make a space large enough for a manhole. Once the locks are fitted, it is important to be meticulous about locking up whenever going out, even for a short period. It is especially easy to forget the vulnerable back door in summer. A key left under the mat, behind a drainpipe or on a piece of string through the letter box is of course an invitation to the dishonest.

Thieves may be put off by knowing your property is marked with your post code and house number, and you can announce the fact with a door or window sticker. Kits can be bought from DIY shops or some police stations. Etching is preferable to ultraviolet marking, which fades and can be removed. You may like to take colour photographs of any special treasures to aid recovery if they are stolen. Check your house contents insurance policy to make sure its cover is up to date.

It helps to ask neighbours to keep an eye on the house if you are away and to make sure free papers and mail are not visible through the letter box. You will of course have stopped delivery of milk and newspapers yourself.

It is obviously foolish to have more than a small, essential sum of money in the house, or to keep cheque cards and cheque books together. A spyhole in the front door makes it easier to identify callers, and a security chain allows their credentials to be checked before letting them in. If in doubt, ring the company or organization the caller claims to represent, or call the police. Women who live alone may prefer to use only their surname and initials in the telephone directory, rather than a first name that reveals their gender.

The police never mind being called by an anxious householder, and it is sensible to do so if you think you hear a prowler outside or have reason to fear on returning home that thieves have entered in your absence.

Crime safety outdoors

Wise pedestrians avoid isolated or poorly lit short cuts, especially at night. Keep your door key in your pocket, separate from any papers with your address on, and carry no more money than you are likely to need. If anyone does try to rob you, do *not* resist – you are much more valuable than anything you own. Some people like to carry a screech alarm in their hands, ready to set off; these can be bought in some DIY shops. You could ask whether there are any self-defence classes for pensioners in your area.

When travelling on public transport, sit with other people. Drivers should park in well-lit places and check around before leaving the vehicle. Have the car keys ready for use on your return, but pause to check that there is no one already in the car before you get in.

If you become a victim of a crime

An intrusion into your home or, worse, an attack on your person is a very distressing experience and you will be understandably upset. Let the police know at once by dialling 999. If your home has been burgled, do not touch anything before the police arrive. Once they have dealt with the urgent practical matters, the police may be able to tell you of a local Victims' Support Group which can help you to cope with your unpleasant experience and get your confidence back.

In fact older people often cope well with this sort of trouble. They have a lifetime's experience of bad times as well as good, and often seem to take a more philosophical attitude to possessions than younger people. Even those who have lost treasured keepsakes often console themselves with the thought that the love they represent remains and cannot be taken away.

Avoiding accidents at home

Falls

Balance and stability tend to deteriorate as the years pass, so that older people are more likely to fall than younger ones. This tendency can be countered by keeping fit, which seems both to increase stability and to strengthen the muscles that help in changing position. Again, common sense and being realistic about any changes in your capabilities often reduce risks without interfering with the normal activity pattern.

Many falls are caused by reckless actions like clambering on to rickety furniture to hang curtains rather than using a solid stepladder. An activity such as changing a light bulb which involves tipping the head back while reaching upwards may cause giddiness: if you find this is so, get someone else to do the job. The mechanisms that direct blood to the brain on sitting or standing upright also become less efficient with age, so too rapid a change of position can lead to faintness and a fall. It is wise to change position slowly, even if the telephone or doorbell is ringing; really important calls will be repeated. Shoes are more stable than slippers, which are best confined to the bedroom. Walking aids such as sticks may become treacherous if their rubber ferrules are worn down. Some chain chemists stock these, but if you have difficulty finding a replacement, ask at your local branch of Age Concern.

Many newly retired people set about putting their home in order for their old age. This makes excellent sense, providing previously deskbound people do not over-estimate their physical abilities.

Repositioning cupboards may eliminate reaching up and bending down that may become difficult later. It also helps to have power points resited from floor level to a point about 3 feet (1 metre) off the floor. As we all become blind to familiar trouble spots, a friend's eyes are useful to help you spot trip hazards such as torn or rucked up carpets, loose stair rods or rugs, low footstools, doorstops and trailing electrical flex. Then make safe all you can.

Frailer people who need equipment like rails beside baths, around lavatories or on stairs, can get advice from the occupational therapist based at the local Social Services Department. For people wanting to find out about the whole range of equipment available to help a disabled person stay independent, either on their own behalf or for a disabled relative or friend, Disabled Living Centres catering for this need can be found in many big cities; a full list of these can be obtained from RADAR (see page 169). The larger chain chemists often keep a stock of simpler aids like non-slip bath mats.

It is sensible for frailer old people to take great care on the stairs, especially if they wear bifocals, which may give misleading visual information. It may help to come downstairs very slowly, letting the second foot join the first on each tread before the lead foot descends to the next stair. Counting the steps makes a stumble over a forgotten stair less likely. Some people feel safer coming downstairs backwards.

Good lighting is a great help to home safety. It is tempting to save money by using low-wattage light bulbs in halls and on stairs, but this is a dangerous false economy. The ageing eye's ability to adapt to dark vision can be poor, so it is very dangerous to walk around even in the most familiar surroundings in the dark or the half-light. Make sure you can reach your bedside light without getting out of bed. Keeping a torch on the bedside table is an extra precaution.

If you experience 'giddy turns' or have fallen without an obvious explanation, it makes sense to consult the doctor, as correction of a small health fault may put things right.

Fire prevention
Fire Officers tell us the most dangerous object in the kitchen is the chip pan. If it does catch fire, it is unsafe to pour water on it; instead, smother the flames with a fire blanket or a damp cloth, turn off the heat and leave the pan to cool. If in any doubt about its safety, call the fire brigade. When leaving the kitchen after a cooking session, it is wise to get into the habit of taking a quick general safety check to make sure that the cooker and electrical appliances are all turned off and all cloths are hung well away from hot objects.

Around the house, make sure electrical appliances are still safe;

danger signs include poor functioning, cutting out or the attached plug getting hot. Old electric fires with exposed elements should be replaced. Check flexes, as they may wear out and need replacing even when the equipment they supply still gives sterling service. Overloading power points by using multiple adaptors can cause a fire as well as the inconvenience of a blown fuse. It goes without saying that appliances' directions for use must be carefully followed; for instance, electric blankets should only be used as overblankets or left on all night if they are designed to do this safely. Old household wiring may be unequal to the load of modern appliances it now serves; if so, it should be replaced.

Open fires should always be damped down before going to bed, while free-standing oil stoves are best not used as they are so easily overturned. It is wise to make sure that trailing garments like dressing gowns, nightdresses and housecoats are made of non-inflammable fabric.

Serious fires are often started by smokers who fall asleep while indulging. All smoking materials must be carefully extinguished, and it is as well to check this has been done before leaving a room. Of course, the safest as well as healthiest thing to do is to stop smoking altogether.

Smoke detectors are battery-powered to set off an alarm if there is something burning in your home. They are usually fitted on the ceiling or high on the wall in a central place such as the hall. They can be especially reassuring to people whose sense of smell is poor.

Safety in the cold

Hypothermia can pose a threat to even the most sensible pensioner. This is because the ability to detect a falling body temperature becomes dulled as the years pass, so that an older person is less aware of the need to turn up heating or put on more clothes. A room thermometer is therefore a necessity, and living room and bedroom temperatures should be maintained above 68°F (20°C). In especially cold weather you may prefer to live in and heat only one room, with the bed pushed against an inside wall. Draw the curtains promptly at dusk to help keep the heat in. Layers of light wool clothing can keep you warm without restricting movement. Frail people who cannot move about much may like to wear a woolly hat, gloves and socks even indoors.

Make winter plans as autumn approaches, checking that all heating appliances are in safe working order. Good insulation helps to minimize heating costs, but make sure your coal or gas heaters are safely ventilated. Get the electric blanket serviced if necessary, and if you prefer a hot water bottle, make sure it is not perished. Check the store cupboard and arrange a good supply of hot food and drinks. Divided saucepans, slow cookers and thermos flasks may be investments that help you make the best use of energy. Make sure your blankets have not worn too thin to be useful, and replace if necessary. Newspaper sandwiched between the layers can help in an emergency. At the onset of winter, organizations like Age Concern and Help the Aged often run special information projects about hypothermia; you may like to watch out for these.

Paying the bills

Your hardworking life may have entitled you to financial benefits you are not claiming. You could check this with Age Concern's annual publication, *Your Rights*, or ask at the local social security office. Some councils help with the costs of insulation and draughtproofing. There may be a local Staying Put or Care and Repair scheme in your area, which gives advice and help in organizing works and the finance to pay for them.

The gas and electricity boards try to help older consumers. If you dislike paying large heating bills in arrears, you may like to ask at the local office about budget accounts and prepayment stamps. It is most important to tell the fuel board concerned *at once* if you receive a bill you cannot pay, as they will not cut off supplies to pensioner households in these circumstances.

Sex and loving

Younger people are surprised and occasionally shocked to discover that older people have sexual feelings and often wish to express them physically. Retired people knew this all along.

Interest in sex varies from one person to another in all age groups, but in general sexual activity up to and including full intercourse should be possible for anyone in normal health. Sex life can even improve in old age, when there may be many years' worth of tenderness and companionship to fuel its expression. Also, circumstances may be more favourable than when life was crowded with work and the demands of children; a siesta or a late breakfast can provide new opportunities when partners are less likely to be overtired than at bedtime.

Normal ageing affects sexual abilities less than is generally supposed. Healthy older men should still have sufficiently firm erections for intercourse to be satisfactory for both parties. Sometimes ejaculation is delayed or does not accompany every orgasm, but this does not represent 'the beginning of the end' for the sex life. True impotence – the inability to have erections – is abnormal and can sometimes be cured, especially when occurring as the unwanted effect of a medicine.

Women sometimes experience problems at and after the time of the menopause, when the level of female hormones falls. The vagina and its lining tissues become less elastic and lubrication takes longer and is less efficient. Mild symptoms can be relieved by KY jelly bought from the chemist, but more severe ones require medical attention. A prescription for a local hormone cream may put things right, or hormone replacement therapy may be helpful.

Threats to sexual activity in later life

Ill health
Many couples stop having sex because the male partner is experiencing potency problems. If they want to continue a sexual

relationship, it is worth finding out whether anything can be done to help. To do this, it is necessary to bring oneself to discuss intimate matters with a professional – not always easy, and not all professionals are helpful. The points to establish with the doctor or nurse are, first, what is likely to be causing the trouble, and second, can anything be done about it? If the family doctor is unable or unwilling to help, he or she may know of a local specialist such as a gynaecologist, urological surgeon, neurologist or psychiatrist who has knowledge and experience in this field.

When professional help is hard to find or when you would like to get further information, SPOD (The Association to Aid the Sexual and Personal Relationships of People with a Disability, see page 170) is a good source of advice and reading matter for both able-bodied and disabled older people. The latter can also be helped by information from the relevant self-help group, such as the Chest, Heart and Stroke Association (see page 168).

When it becomes impossible to use sexual techniques to which you are accustomed, it sometimes helps to consider whether pleasure and fulfilment could be derived from doing something different. Of course, anything two adults do together which both enjoy and which hurts neither is a legitimate expression of affection; there is nothing 'kinky' about hand-to-genital contact, mouth-to-genital contact or the use of any position in which sexual activity is easier and more comfortable. Though people are quite capable of working this out for themselves, 'permission' from a professional sometimes makes them feel better about it.

Loss of a partner
Although this affects both sexes, wives are more often left alone than husbands. Whereas the sexes are equal in number at age fifty-five, there are two women to every man aged sixty-five and three to every man of eighty. As women also tend to marry men who are older than they are, there are many more elderly widows than widowers, and a shortage of male companions and sexual partners in later life.

Someone whose partner has died is expected to feel bereaved, but the sexual element of the very complex feelings experienced is seldom discussed. Once the acute pain of loss has passed, sexual frustration adds another misery to the daily dreariness of adjustment. Some people use masturbation to relieve physical tension and loneliness. This is fine if it helps, and of course does no physical or mental harm. Emotional energy also requires an outlet; people without families to care for often compensate by finding other people who need looking after – a very sensible form of adaptation. Talking to someone you trust also helps. Suggestions for further reading about sexual and other relationships can be found in the book list.

Older homosexuals naturally feel the same sort of loss as a widow or widower when their partner of many years dies, and people in general are starting to realize this. The Gay Bereavement Project may be a useful contact (see page 169).

Attitudes of others

Why do younger people find it so difficult to accept that their elders are sexual beings? A number of factors seem to be involved. We all seem to think that sex is reserved for 'people like us', of our age and orientation and in similar circumstances; outside our group, sex is not quite decent. Many of us have sexual difficulties of our own, and it can be very threatening to discover that someone much older is more successful sexually than we are. The advertising media imply that love and romance is confined to young, glamorous users of their product – obvious nonsense, but too pervasive to ignore. Our refusal to accept our parents' sexuality is particularly complex. Incest taboos, memories of childhood punishments for 'dirty' talk or behaviour, grief for a lost parent and fear for a threatened inheritance if the surviving partner remarries are often mixed up together.

Older people may need to be fairly robust in defending their human right to sexual expression against the onslaught of suddenly prim younger relatives. A little finesse helps, plus a lot of consideration for any tender spots in the young person's private life, for few of us are entirely comfortable about our sexuality.

Stress, worry and mental health

Coping with stress

No life can be stress-free. In retirement as at other times circumstances can be difficult. Instead of toning up the system just enough to meet the challenge, stress can produce enough strain to be harmful. When this happens it is easy to drink too much, resort to tranquillizers or binge on food. Far from helping, this adds a new problem to those that set the cycle off.

The amount and type of stress which can be withstood varies from person to person, and also changes from one time to another in a single individual. Older people have a lifetime's experience of overcoming difficulties, and given reasonable health, often cope better than younger ones. A decision to take charge of life is wise: feeling the powerless victim of circumstances can lead to depression. Taking stock of difficulties reveals two sorts of problem: those that can possibly be solved and those that probably cannot. The first category will include practical problems like unsuitable housing, poor health and insufficient money. Various kinds of help are available, some described elsewhere in this book. Even if you have tried to put things right before and failed, it may be worth trying again, as new services or treatment may have been introduced since your last attempt. Good places to start asking include the Citizens' Advice Bureau, Community Health Council and your local branch of Age Concern, while Age Concern England and Help the Aged produce a wide range of publications on topics that concern retired people (see pages 167 and 169).

Having put right everything possible, putting up with the rest may be more difficult in retirement than formerly. Domestic problems loom larger without the distraction of work, resilience may be temporarily weakened by the shock of life change, and natural interventionists may find resignation no easier with the passage of time.

Being too close to the problem may distort the view. It may

help to restore perspective by talking things over with a trusted outsider.

Greater contact with the outside world through a new interest or activity or a return to an old one can help to restore a sense of proportion. Carers are sometimes enabled to do this if their duties can be taken over for a time by a substitute like a Crossroads Care Attendant. She or he is a trained person who relieves the carer of her or his responsibilities for a while, and can work flexible hours to cover either regular or emergency needs. The Crossroads Care Attendants Schemes started from the TV programme. There are now over 100 locally based schemes, funded partly by donations and partly by statutory money. Their great value is their flexibility and the fact that they will do things the carer's way – altogether a very bright and innovative scheme. See page 168 for the address of the Association's head office.

Physical exercise often helps a lot, channelling energy and attention to the working muscles and giving a pleasant sense of well-being and healthy tiredness at the end of the day.

Learning to relax
It may be worth making the effort to learn some simple relaxation techniques. Various commercial tapes and books are available, but the essentials are described below.

1. *Loosening the muscles*. Begin by clenching your fists and tightening all your muscles for a count of three. Then let go, relaxing the tension and letting all your muscles go loose. Once you know what this feels like, relax even further, starting at your toes and working upwards.
2. *Breathing*. Take slow, regular breaths in through your nose and out through your mouth.
3. *Images*. When you are relaxed and have steadied your breathing, call up a restful picture in your mind's eye – of a quiet scene or a favourite activity.

Avoiding depression
Feeling low after retirement often comes as a surprise – why

should all that freedom seem so dreary? People sometimes overlook the losses that come at this time – of job and status, the company of workmates, the pattern to the day. Women who have worked in the home also have to adjust their routine to include a newly present husband, and this can cause unexpected friction. The disturbed pieces of life normally settle into a new pattern, but careful thought followed by positive action can shorten the process and reduce the trauma.

Various strategies help to prevent low spirits. Keeping busy helps; stepping down the old job gradually or taking a new part-time one may cushion the shock. Voluntary work involving contact with other people is especially good for morale; charities, political parties or religious organizations usually have openings for volunteers. Some people like to extend their education through day or evening classes or the Open University. The University of the Third Age (see page 170), specifically for older people, provides a network of local groups who learn by a self-help process. There are also many residential courses, some held in beautiful surroundings. Some Age Concern branches have Skills Centres where older people pass on their knowledge of crafts to younger ones. Keeping busy on your own takes motivation, but some people like to develop a lifetime's interest in gardening, art or handicrafts.

After being a 'manager' throughout adult life, it can often be difficult to admit to a need for help yourself. Having a confidant has been found, unsurprisingly, to promote mental health; we all need to 'debrief' and shed life's minor irritations as well as major troubles. The fortunate can find a listening ear at home or among close friends, and often the relationship is mutually supportive. Others resort to professionals such as clergy, doctors and members of organizations like Relate (formerly the Marriage Guidance Council) and the Samaritans: this last exists to help anyone who is troubled, not just those contemplating suicide.

Bad health is very lowering; it is always worth making sure it is as good as possible. A good clear-out of the bathroom cupboard may yield a harvest of tablet bottles. If these are taken to the doctor, medication can be fully reviewed and reduced to the bare minimum. Sight and hearing are important for independence, and some body maintenance (see below) may be in order.

A lifetime of work followed by a retirement of social service can sound a little over-earnest. People need pleasure; it is sensible mental hygiene to arrange a small 'treat' for oneself every day, with something bigger to look forward to every week or so.

Leaving paid employment almost always reduces social contact. It can be easy to become isolated unless a conscious effort is made to keep up with the closest workmates, to renew contact with old friends or to make new ones.

Small losses like these are easier to cope with than big ones like the death of a partner. Nothing can remove the pain of a bereavement, or replace the loss. Not everyone has the comfort of family and friends at this time, and extra support can be gained from organizations like Cruse, the National Association of Widows or the Gay Bereavement Project (see pages 168–70).

A few people have so much to bear that they contemplate ending their lives. Sometimes these feelings occur as part of a depressive illness, which can be treated. Depressed people may be unable to organize help for themselves, so it is vitally important to notify the doctor without delay if someone you know is threatening suicide; these threats may be acted on.

Most of us seem to have a need to find meaning in our lives. For an older person this can often mean reflecting on the past, reminiscing with others and sometimes revisiting old haunts. Some people find becoming reconciled with estranged friends or family members helps their peace of mind. Religion is a support to some, and old beliefs and practices may resume their past importance. Others find the contemplation of natural beauty, the rhythm of the seasons or of great art and literature a necessary complement to their own experience. Time spent finding one's own peace in one's own way is not time wasted.

Essential body maintenance

Regular checks on eyes, teeth and feet help to keep them working well and enable abnormalities to be treated at an early stage.

Eyes

The only important 'normal' change in the eye with age is the decline in the focussing power of the lens, so that spectacles are needed to read small print. Other changes are not normal and may be signs that urgent treatment is needed. The following symptoms should be reported to a doctor or eye hospital *at once*:

- Sudden loss of vision, even if it returns on its own.
- Disturbance of the field of vision – black patches appearing in it, or an apparent shutter or curtain blocking part of it.
- Seeing flashing lights, or the appearance of coloured haloes around lamps.
- Pain and redness of the eye.

A routine examination is also sensible for problem-free eyes. This can detect sight-threatening conditions such as glaucoma at an early stage and thus minimize eye damage. People without eye symptoms and who have noticed no change in their vision should have an eye test every two years. An eye test is free for pensioners who:

- have glaucoma or are closely related to a glaucoma sufferer;
- suffer from diabetes;
- are on low incomes, in some cases (see Social Security Leaflet G11, from your social security office or post office).

Other pensioners pay a fee.

Good lighting makes the most of sight. Older people in particular benefit from a good reading light – 60 watts in a flexible holder directed over the shoulder.

Teeth

Bad teeth can worsen health when a soft, unhealthy diet is followed because of inability to chew fibre-rich foods. Bad

permanent teeth may become unsightly, while uncomfortable
dentures may be left out, giving their non-wearer an unattractive
'gummy' appearance.

The major threat to teeth from adult life onwards is plaque
(tartar), a sticky deposit on or between teeth. If allowed to build
up, it causes gum disease and eventually damages the teeth
themselves. This can be avoided if the plaque is removed by
regular brushing and flossing. A check-up at the dentist every six
months provides an opportunity for thorough professional clean-
ing and for prompt attention to faults.

People with full dentures should see the dentist annually to
make sure their teeth still fit and to have the health of the mouth
itself checked. Even serious conditions like cancer of the mouth
lining are usually curable if diagnosed and treated promptly.

A fact sheet on *Dental Care in Retirement* which includes up-
to-date information on payment is available from Age Concern
England.

Feet

It is worth taking the time and trouble to find comfortable shoes
that fit well – not always an easy task. Feet sometimes spread in
later life, so your size may change in width, length or both. If you
have trouble finding a supplier, you could write to the Society of
Shoe Fitters, ask a chiropodist or inquire at a Disabled Living
Centre. Excess weight causes extra strain on the feet as well as the
weightbearing joints above them, so painful feet may benefit from
a change in eating habits.

Many older people have trouble cutting their toenails if their
joint mobility or eyesight is less than perfect. There may be a nail-
cutting service in your area; the local Age Concern branch or
Social Services Department should know. Corns and callouses
can be kept at bay to some extent by rubbing in E45 cream,
available from the chemist. If they do develop, it is better to see a
chiropodist rather than to attempt surgery yourself, as elderly feet
tend to have a poor blood supply and therefore to heal less well.

Chiropody under the NHS is free to people over sixty-five, but waiting lists for treatment are long in some areas. If you decide to seek private treatment, make sure the chiropodist is state-registered. Regular chiropody is essential for diabetics. This is because diabetes interferes with the healing process and also impairs sensation, so it is easy for a sore place on a diabetic foot to develop and worsen unnoticed. Six-monthly treatment is usually recommended, but you should go at once if you notice a change in skin colour or a sore place. It is also worth checking footwear for possible sources of damage like cracks or creases in the leather and protruding nails.

Sense about health checks

Medical examinations of healthy people are only useful when they detect a serious, treatable condition at a stage in its development when it would otherwise be unnoticed.

The potential benefits of such testing are offset by some obvious drawbacks. Identifying people with such a condition is still useless unless effective treatment is available. Some testing procedures are uncomfortable or unpleasant in themselves. Sometimes a 'false positive' result can cause a great deal of needless distress before it can be shown to be a mistake. Tests also cost money and use resources that might be employed elsewhere.

Balancing benefits against human and financial costs, experts in general agree that the three sorts of check described below are probably worth the trouble and expense. The first two are for women only.

Cervical smear

This detects changes in the cells of the neck of the womb that may later progress to cancer. An internal (vaginal) examination is necessary for the cell sample to be scraped off the cervix. Women past the menopause sometimes find the procedure uncomfortable.

Smears are recommended for all sexually active women every three years up to the age of sixty-five. These are available free under the NHS from the GP or at the Well Woman Clinic. After sixty-five, if you have never had a smear it is wise to ask if you can have one done, even if you are no longer sexually active. If you have previously had smear tests, you should ask your doctor's advice as you approach the age of sixty-five; if your smear results have previously been normal, your risk may now be so low as to render further smears unnecessary.

Mammography

Breast cancer is still the commonest cancer among women in England, though lung cancer is overtaking it in frequency. A mammogram is a sort of x-ray which can detect breast cancer at an early and treatable stage, when it is too small to be felt by an examining hand. Mammography requires a special x-ray machine installed in a hospital or a special screening centre. NHS policy is that women aged between fifty and sixty-four should have free mammography every three years. When the service starts in their area women over sixty-five may like to ask the doctor whether they should have one too.

Monthly breast self-examination is also useful to detect slightly larger lumps – perhaps 1 cm (½ inch) across or larger. However they are detected, all lumps need biopsy to find out whether or not they are cancerous. This means that part of the lump is removed to be examined under a microscope. A biopsy may be done in the Outpatients' Clinic using a needle and syringe, or may involve a small operation under anaesthetic, with an overnight stay in hospital.

If you cannot find out how to get these tests from your doctor or the Secretary of the Community Health Council, the Women's National Cancer Control Campaign may be able to help (see page 170).

Measurements of blood pressure (BP)

We all have 'blood pressure', which is the force that keeps the blood circulating round the body. During middle life and the early retirement years, a person whose blood pressure is higher than normal runs an increased risk of having a stroke. This risk can be reduced by taking regular medication to lower the BP, but the medicines sometimes have undesirable effects. The discomfort and inconvenience they cause have to be balanced against the possible benefits in each case.

It seems sensible to have the BP checked every five years up to the age of seventy-five. This often gets done as part of a general medical examination or as a spot check when visiting the surgery for another reason. If you are under seventy-five and have not had your BP measured recently, you would be wise to ask the doctor to do this for you. After the age of seventy-five the situation becomes much less clear-cut, as the ill effects of lowering the BP often outweigh its possible benefits. An individual decision on whether or not to treat has to be made in each case.

When to see the doctor
It is wise to see the doctor whenever a health problem is interfering with your independence and restricting your activities. For instance, faulty bladder control or a tendency to fall should not be allowed to continue uninvestigated and untreated. When available, a health visitor can be a very useful person to talk to if your difficulties seem to be a complex mixture of physical, mental and social factors which you would like help in disentangling.

Some symptoms should be discussed with the doctor as soon as possible, even if they are not serious in themselves. Almost always an innocent explanation is found for them. Occasionally, however, prompt action means that a serious illness like cancer can be dealt with at an early and treatable stage. See the doctor promptly if you notice:

- a lump in the breast;
- an ulcer that will not heal on your skin or in your mouth;
- bleeding from the back passage, blood streaks in spit or a bloodstained discharge from the vagina;
- hoarseness persisting for more than three weeks;
- a persistent cough, especially if you are a smoker.

Some people who later suffer a stroke have a warning beforehand. This takes the form of transient stroke symptoms, which come on within minutes and rapidly get better, often before the hastily summoned doctor can arrive. This is called a transient ischaemic attack (TIA). The sufferer may experience weakness or loss of feeling in part of his body, or speech impairment, or he may become confused. Someone who suffers a TIA should consult the doctor at once; if the cause can be found on investigation, the threatened major stroke can be avoided.

Some cases of permanent blindness could be prevented if prompt action were taken on similar warning signs affecting the eye. Common complaints include loss or severe impairment of all or part of the visual field, which may recover spontaneously. Sufferers from giant cell arteritis, a curable condition of the blood vessels which can threaten sight if left untreated, may have severe headaches and tenderness of the face and scalp as well as visual problems (see page 68).

*

People of whatever age have a right to choose their own lifestyle. The information in this section is there so the choice can be informed. There is evidence that cultivating healthy living habits can increase wellbeing in the later years, rather than just prolonging dependency. The object of the exercise is to 'die young, as late as possible'.

Common Illnesses of Later Life

While illness in old age is not of course 'normal', many older people have ailments which in the case of an unlucky few can interfere with the way they want to live their lives. This chapter describes the common illnesses of later life and outlines what can be done about them. Further details of drug treatment will be found in the relevant section of the chapter on medicines. The conditions are arranged according to the body systems they affect, except for cancers, which are discussed together.

One note of warning: you would be most unwise to use this chapter to diagnose and treat yourself: attempting to do this often causes unnecessary worry and can even be dangerous. Instead, the information here is intended to boost your confidence in discussing your health problems and their management with your doctors. You have a right to know what is happening to your body, and most doctors are glad to give information to patients who show an intelligent interest in their care. Many people find it helps to read up the subject beforehand and to make a list of their particular questions and concerns. This avoids the frustration of only remembering the really vital point when you are halfway home again.

Just as each person and illness is different, so the best treatment varies from case to case, and a short book like this cannot list all the possible alternatives. Local circumstances will also affect which parts of your treatment your GP will undertake himself and which you will receive at the hospital. If you are a fit pensioner, you should not feel insulted if a consultation with a geriatrician is suggested. This doctor is an expert on the diseases of older bodies just as a paediatrician has specialist knowledge about younger ones, and the 'whole person' approach of the geriatrician can often be most helpful to an older patient. Geriatric units designed for assessment and rehabilitation of people like yourself are usually busy, cheerful places, and you are likely to be pleasantly surprised by what you find.

Most illnesses respond best if managed by a partnership of patient and doctor working together. Also most people, whether sick or well, prefer to take control of their lives, rather than feeling they are the pawn of experts, however kindly and well-intentioned. Helping yourself is therefore very important, and suggestions for ways in which you can do this are included in every discussion of treatment. One possibility is to get in touch with the relevant self-help group. These offer information, publications, mutual support and company and, in some cases, practical help. They are mentioned in the text where appropriate, and their addresses are listed at the back of the book.

The heart and blood vessels

The heart is a muscular pump which circulates the blood round the body through the blood vessels (arteries and veins). Because it works hard and unceasingly, the heart needs a good blood supply to provide it with oxygen. This flows through the coronary arteries.

Common problems

ANGINA
The tight, squeezing chest pain of angina occurs because narrowed coronary arteries reduce the blood-borne oxygen supply to the heart muscle. The pain, sometimes accompanied by breathlessness, is often brought on by exercise or emotion. These increase the heart's need for oxygen, while resting lowers the need and usually takes away the pain.

How your doctor can help Having decided you have angina, he can prescribe drugs to help. Several different types are used, given in different ways. You *must* take yours exactly as prescribed (see Chapter 3). Coronary bypass surgery is occasionally performed in fit elderly people whose angina interferes with their active lives. You might want to discuss this possibility with your doctor.

Helping yourself If you are a smoker, stop now, and lose weight if you need to. By doing so you can decrease the strain on your heart. Keep as active as possible within the limits of your pain, as this helps to open up the coronary blood vessels.

HEART ATTACKS

Other names for these are 'coronary thrombosis' or 'myocardial infarct'. Heart attacks occur when part of the heart muscle dies because its blood supply is too poor to keep it alive. A young or middle-aged person with a coronary has a tight or crushing pain which often spreads into his neck and arms. He is often breathless and distressed and may become unconscious. An elderly person sometimes experiences pain like this, but does not always do so. Instead he may faint, fall, vomit or become confused.

How your doctor can help He may take an electrocardiogram (ECG) to help him make his diagnosis. If you are in pain he will give you painkillers and may add an injection to help open up the blocked coronary vessel. In discussion with you and your relatives he will decide whether you should best be looked after at home or in hospital. In either place a tailor-made treatment plan will be worked out for you. This will include drugs to control any symptoms and also a gradual return to activity. You may be given long-term medication to prevent further heart attacks.

Helping yourself Try to be as optimistic as you can. Heart attacks are not trivial, but many people have survived them to continue to enjoy productive lives. Discuss your lifestyle with your doctor and think carefully about it if he thinks your should alter a stressful existence. If you smoke, you should stop at once; this will make you fitter now and reduce your chances of a further attack. Try not to overload your heart by gaining weight. Moderate exercise is very good for you, and there may be a special exercise programme for heart attack sufferers in your area. You should avoid actions involving violent, sudden strain, such as moving furniture, push-starting cars or shovelling snow. The Chest, Heart and Stroke Association produces leaflets about heart attacks that you may find helpful. See page 168.

DISORDERS OF HEART RHYTHM
These are quite common and not always serious. The sufferer may complain of palpitations, an uncomfortable awareness of the heart-beat, or notice nothing abnormal. More serious rhythm disorders can cause breathlessness, falls or attacks of unconsciousness.

How your doctor can help His first task is to identify the rhythm disorder. This is done by recording an electrocardiogram (ECG), either on a single occasion or over a twenty-four-hour period using a body-worn tape recorder. You will probably need to attend the hospital for further tests and may see a heart specialist (a cardiologist). Your treatment will probably involve drug therapy or the implantation of a pacemaker. This is a simple electrical device consisting of a battery with a wire to conduct an electrical impulse to the heart and so stimulate it to beat. Pacemakers sometimes save lives. More often, they prevent falls and breathlessness and make an active life possible again.

Helping yourself Take your medicines exactly as directed. If you have a pacemaker, remember that problems with them are rare but if they occur you should report to the hospital pacemaker clinic as quickly as possible. Check how often you will need a new battery and whether your particular device will be affected by equipment such as microwave ovens or electronic security checks at airports.

HIGH BLOOD PRESSURE
Doctors sometimes refer to this as hypertension. People with a

higher than average blood pressure in middle life seem to be more likely than others to have heart attacks, strokes or failing kidneys. Measures to lower high blood pressure in this age group make good sense. In the case of retired people the situation is much less clear, and doctors hold differing opinions as to what level of blood pressure, if any, requires treatment.

How your doctor can help He can check your blood pressure at regular intervals (at least every five years) up to the age of seventy-five. If you are already taking blood pressure-lowering medicines, he will probably want to see you every few months. He may decrease your dose or stop the drugs altogether as you get older.

Helping yourself Make sure you attend for your regular check-ups and discuss your treatment with your doctor. See him promptly if your medicines seem to be upsetting you, for instance if you become unsteady on your feet, very tired, have trouble controlling your urine, experience problems with your sex life or become less clear mentally. These symptoms nearly always get better if the offending drugs are stopped.

ARTERIAL DISEASE

In the commonest type the leg arteries become too narrow to supply enough blood to the muscles. This causes pain in the calf on walking which gets better with rest. (Doctors call this intermittent claudication.) Patients with more severe disease get pain even at rest, and it may wake them from sleep, getting better if they hang the leg out of bed. Their toes may be tender to touch and troubled by 'pins and needles'. In the very worst cases the blood supply becomes insufficient to keep the tissues healthy, so ulcers and eventually gangrene develop.

How your doctor can help He will probably order some tests to find out about the condition of your blood and its circulation. An ultrasound examination of your leg may be performed to locate the blockage; this is quite painless and involves no injections.

Once he has the test results, he can treat any conditions such as anaemia or diabetes that are worsening your symptoms. He will give you painkillers if you need them. If your pain on walking is not getting worse, he will be able to reassure you that you are unlikely to need surgery in the future and are very unlikely to develop gangrene.

If your disease is a little more severe, you may have pain at rest. Surgery is advisable in some cases, and special x-rays called arteriograms will be taken first. Under a local anaesthetic a special dye is injected into the artery, and the picture this gives of the blockage and its surroundings helps the surgeon to plan your treatment.

The operation offered to you will depend on the circumstances of your case. A lumbar sympathectomy, which can be done under local anaesthetic, blocks the action of the nerves that narrow the blood vessels. It can give useful relief for up to three years. Direct arterial operations are also used, and the vessel may be rebored, stretched or its narrowed section bypassed by a graft.

Helping yourself Stopping smoking will prevent your symptoms from getting worse. You should take great care of your feet, which will be slow to heal even after minor injury. Choose new shoes carefully, to avoid damage to fragile skin; a heel ½ inch (1 cm) higher than usual will relax the calf muscle and may help your pain. Wash and dry your feet carefully every day and avoid extremes of heat and cold. It is sensible to visit a chiropodist regularly.

VARICOSE VEINS AND ULCERS
The veins carry blood from the tissues back to the heart. Normal veins have valves shaped like pockets with their openings towards the heart, and these prevent the blood from running backwards. A varicose vein is wider and longer than a normal one and takes a more winding course. Its valves cannot work properly because of the change in shape, and this accounts for some of the symptoms. Sufferers complain of swelling and aching discomfort in the leg, as well as the unsightly appearance. The veins may become infected (phlebitis) or may bleed profusely if injured.

People with severe varicose veins can develop swelling, stiffening and pigmentation of their leg tissues, which eventually break down to form an ulcer. These usually occur on the inner surface of the leg, just above the ankle. Itching eczema around the ulcer is common.

How your doctor can help Surgery is sometimes possible for varicose veins, but is more commonly performed in younger patients. The veins may be injected to clot and shrink them, or they can be removed altogether. Your doctor is more likely to advise the use of elastic stockings, which he can prescribe.

For very severe varicose ulcers the doctor may suggest a period of bed rest, perhaps in hospital. Occasionally a skin graft is advisable. He is much more likely to suggest pressure bandaging, and he will ask the practice or district nurse to do this. Several different types of pressure bandage are in use, changed at intervals when the ulcer is cleaned and dressed. Healing is slow but can usually be achieved in two to three months. The skin can then be kept intact by the correct use of elastic stockings.

Helping yourself If you are given elastic stockings, make sure you use them correctly: keep them on your bedside table and put them on before you get out of bed. Try to persevere with their use if you find them a little uncomfortable at first.

Follow your doctor's advice about rest and exercise. Walking is usually recommended, as it keeps the blood flowing through the veins and helps to disperse fluid from the swollen leg.

You should avoid spending long periods standing. When sitting, put your feet up sufficiently high for the blood from your feet to flow downhill to your bottom: low, dainty footstools are useless.

If you are overweight, losing the excess may help.

The lungs and airways

These take oxygen into the body, where it is needed to burn up food for heat and energy. As the chest expands when breathing in, air rushes down the airways into the lungs. Here oxygen from the air crosses a thin membrane to reach the blood, which carries it round the body. At the same time the waste product carbon dioxide passes back from the blood into the lungs and is breathed out as the chest contracts to its resting position.

Common problems

COLDS

These are due to infection by viruses. A dry, sore throat and sneezing are followed by discharge from the nose, which becomes thick. A cold should get better within a week to ten days.

How your doctor can help Medicine can do little for an uncomplicated cold. Antibiotics are ineffective against viruses, and there is no effective cold vaccine.

Consult your doctor if your cold develops complications such as a chest infection or if it is slow to go away.

Helping yourself Try not to spread your cold around. If possible, keep away from other people during the early sneezing stage when it is most infectious. Careful handwashing also helps to prevent spread.

Take aspirin or paracetamol for discomfort, gargling with crushed or dissolved tablets to help a sore throat. Never take aspirin on an empty stomach. It is not necessary to 'feed a cold' if you do not feel like large meals, but be sure to take 4–5 pints of fluid a day. You may find lemon or blackcurrant drinks or hot toddies comforting. Steam inhalations help to clear sticky mucus, but care is needed to avoid scalds. Scented additions to the hot water are not necessary.

'FLU

Many so-called cases of 'flu are in fact bad colds or other respiratory infections. True influenza is comparatively rare. It tends to occur in epidemics. The illness is more severe than a cold, with a high temperature, head and muscle aches and often a period of depression during convalescence.

How your doctor can help Antibiotics cannot kill the virus but may be useful if bacterial infection follows it. 'Flu injections to prevent infection with the prevailing germ become available at the start of an epidemic.

Helping yourself Ask your doctor for a 'flu injection at the beginning of winter if you suffer from heart or chest problems.

When you have 'flu, pain relief and plenty of fluids may help. 'Flu is likely to make you feel worse for longer than a cold does, so you may need to accept extra, temporary help from friends, neighbours and Social Services.

Consult your doctor if you feel very unwell during the acute illness or have not recovered within two to three weeks.

CHEST INFECTIONS

These are named according to the part of the breathing apparatus affected by the inflammation ('-itis'). Tracheitis affects the windpipe and causes a cough and soreness behind the breastbone, while bronchitis involves large lung airways and results in a cough with a lot of green or yellow phlegm. Inflammation of the lung substance itself is called pneumonitis or pneumonia. This may cause a cough with spit and chest pain, but in some very elderly people pneumonia is difficult to spot as they may simply become mentally muddled and less able to look after themselves. Chest infections may occur out of the blue but more commonly follow colds or 'flu.

How your doctor can help Antibiotics can kill the bacteria which cause most chest infections. If you develop a cough which lasts longer than two weeks or which produces green or yellow spit, you should see your doctor, who will be able to treat you with antibiotics and any other medicines that may be necessary.

Helping yourself Steam inhalations will again be useful. A hot drink first thing in the morning seems to help to clear the chest, and you should continue to take plenty of fluids through the day. Stay in the warm until you feel better, and make sure your bedroom is heated at night, as cold air worsens coughing.

The digestive system

This consists of a long muscular tube running from the mouth to the opening of the back passage; it includes the throat, stomach, small and large intestines, together with glands such as the liver and pancreas which pass digestive juices into the tube. It processes food into a form in which it can be absorbed into the blood and used in the body for energy, maintenance and growth. Undigested food, bacteria, bile and intestinal juices are passed out as stools.

Common problems

DIVERTICULAR DISEASE

This is sometimes called diverticulosis. It is a very common condition, especially in people who do not take enough fibre in their diet. This means the bowel muscle does not have a residue of undigested food to squeeze against, so the pressure within it becomes high. Pockets of its lining membrane are forced outwards through the muscle and its covering like the inner tube ballooning through a bicycle tyre, and these pockets are called diverticula.

Many people with diverticular disease have no symptoms at all. Others develop pain on the left side of the abdomen with constipation or less often diarrhoea. Occasionally a diverticulum becomes infected (diverticulitis), which in the unlucky few can progress to abscess formation, peritonitis or bowel blockage with severe symptoms of abdominal pain and sickness. This is, however, very unusual. Most patients with diverticular disease can be reassured that their condition is a nuisance rather than a danger and is not likely to shorten their lives.

How your doctor can help He can identify the important and serious causes of abdominal pain and vomiting. You should call him if you have these symptoms and they do not settle within a very few hours. If he thinks you have diverticular disease he may refer you to the hospital for tests, after which he may prescribe medicines or a diet.

Helping yourself A high-fibre diet will help to stop you developing diverticular disease or keep symptoms at bay if you already have it. Ask your doctor to refer you to a dietitian if you have trouble finding a diet you can follow.

HAEMORRHOIDS

These are commonly known as piles. They happen when the lining of the back passage slips down, swells and sometimes bleeds. The bright red blood from piles comes after the stool and usually stains the toilet paper. Itching and soreness round the back passage are common. Piles that cannot be replaced or which develop blood clots are very painful.

Piles tend to run in families and are commoner in people who suffer with constipation.

How your doctor can help He can examine your back passage to confirm that piles are the cause of the trouble. If he is not certain of this he may refer you to the hospital for further examination. Treatment of mild cases involves curing constipation and using a local ointment or cream. More severe cases may need injections or surgery.

Helping yourself Again, a high fibre diet can help prevent piles. You *must* tell your doctor if you pass blood from your back passage. Most cases are due to piles, but a few are caused by bowel cancer which can be cured if treated early enough (see page 93).

PEPTIC ULCER

These happen when acid stomach juice attacks and starts to digest the lining of the stomach and duodenum, which is the part of the intestine leading out of the stomach. This causes abdominal pain, which tends to be worse before meals or during the night when there is no food in the stomach to mop up the acid. The ulcer may give trouble for days or weeks until it heals up, when the patient may be well for some time until symptoms recur. Rarely, complications may develop. The ulcer may erode into a blood vessel, so that the person vomits blood, or perforate and leak stomach contents into the abdominal cavity. This causes severe pain.

No one knows why ulcers happen. Stress, smoking, pain-relieving drugs used for arthritis and excessive coffee and alcohol may worsen their symptoms.

How your doctor can help If he thinks you have an ulcer he may order hospital tests. These may include a barium meal, when you will drink a white liquid to outline your stomach lining on x-ray pictures. Alternatively, you may have a gastroscopy, when the hospital doctor will look at the inside of your stomach through a special telescope passed down your gullet. Your treatment is likely to involve drugs that help your stomach lining to protect itself against acid and thus heal the ulcer. An operation is occasionally necessary for very severe or complicated ulcers.

Helping yourself If you still smoke you should stop, as this will help your ulcer to heal. Alcohol irritates the stomach, so it is sensible to keep your intake well within health guidelines (see Chapter 1). You should be able to take a normal diet, avoiding any food you know upsets you. Smaller, more frequent meals will probably suit you better than larger ones taken less frequently.

HERNIA

A hernia happens when a loop of gut slips into the wrong position. There are several common types:

Inguinal hernia

This is commonly called a rupture. The bowel loop pushes out of the abdominal cavity into the groin, producing a swelling in the scrotum in a man and the labium in a woman. (Each labium forms a fold of flesh on either side of the vaginal opening.) The lump gets bigger when the patient strains or coughs and may become uncomfortable by the end of the day. People with hernias may be able to reduce them by lying down and pressing on the swelling, when the loop of bowel pops back into the abdomen with a gurgle.

A neglected hernia may become stuck (irreducible) and the trapped bowel loop is then in danger from loss of its blood supply. This causes abdominal pain and vomiting, and urgent treatment is required.

The best treatment for an inguinal hernia is surgery to reduce the hernia and then block its exit path. When the patient is unwilling or unfit for surgery, a truss is supplied.

How your doctor can help He can identify a hernia as the cause of the swelling and then refer you to hospital for surgery or the provision of a truss.

Helping yourself Do not smoke; you will then be less likely to get a cough and a subsequent hernia.

If you are prescribed a truss, make sure you are shown how to use it. A truss should be put on before getting out of bed so that the pressure pad blocks the exit tunnel and stops the bowel loop from slipping out. It should then be kept on until bedtime.

Incisional hernia
This happens when the abdominal wall has been weakened by an operation scar and the muscles have not grown together properly underneath it. A loop of bowel can then slip out through the gap to form a soft swelling under the skin which can usually be pushed back into the belly. Small hernias of this sort do not usually need treatment. Surgery is reserved for large ones and those shaped so that the bowel loop may get stuck.

How your doctor can help He can advise you as to whether your incisional hernia needs treatment. If so he can refer you to the hospital for surgery or for a body belt to control the hernia.

Helping yourself An incisional hernia is most likely to develop after an operation in an overweight patient who has a smoker's cough and strains at stool because he is constipated. Eating plenty of fibre and avoiding weight-gain will protect you.

Hiatus hernia

This happens entirely out of sight within the body when part of the stomach slips upwards through the diaphragm. Many patients with hiatus hernia have no symptoms at all. Others have reflux oesophagitis because stomach acid irritates the unprotected gullet lining. This sore area may bleed, causing anaemia, or become narrow so that food cannot pass it.

How your doctor can help He may prescribe treatment himself or send you to the hospital for tests. The most likely are the inspection of your gullet lining with a modified telescope or a barium swallow x-ray. Treatment may involve tablets to reduce the amount of stomach acid and thus prevent irritation of the gullet. Alternatively, the sore area can be coated with a special protective liquid taken after meals.

Helping yourself Raising the head of your bed on blocks will prevent acid stomach contents from 'running uphill' to irritate the sore gullet. This can also be reduced by losing excess weight.

STOMAS

A stoma is an opening on the abdominal wall through which the bowel empties into a bag. The commonest sort in elderly people is the colostomy. This may be necessary if the normal stool pathway needs to be removed during surgery for bowel cancer. Other sorts of stoma are the ileostomy, when the opening is made higher up the bowel, and the urostomy when urine is drained to the outside world via a bowel loop. Temporary colostomies are occasionally made to allow an injured or diseased bowel time to heal before the normal pattern is restored. A permanent colostomy remains for the rest of the patient's life.

How your doctor can help Unless your illness requires emergency treatment, the surgeon will discuss the reasons for the colostomy with you and your family before the operation. You are also likely to meet a stoma care nurse. She specializes in the care of people like yourself, and has an expert and up-to-date knowledge of stoma equipment. Often the hospital will ask a patient who already has a stoma to visit you. You will probably be surprised at how active and normal a life can be enjoyed despite a stoma.

The opening for the stoma has to be formed separately from the operation incision and away from bones, scars and skin creases. If your surgeon knows about your hobbies and activities and what clothes you like to wear he can take these factors into consideration as well. A correctly sited stoma should be inconspicuous with the bag in place, and the bag should not get in the way.

Helping yourself After the operation you will learn how to manage your stoma. A bag and belt system is often used, but with some colostomies it is possible to wash out the bowel every so often and use a cap dressing instead of bags between times. This irrigation technique is not suitable for everyone, however. Before you leave hospital you should make sure you know how to get in touch with your stoma care nurse in case you need advice. It is also sensible to make contact with the appropriate self-help organization, the British Colostomy Association or the Ileostomy Association.

Once home, coping with bag changing will be easier if you organize your bathroom appropriately. It helps if you have a washbasin in the same room as the lavatory, and a chair or stool to sit on is useful. Make sure the room is well lit. It will be convenient if there is room for a cupboard to contain spare bags and belts, adhesive, covers and other kit; otherwise a small suitcase will help to keep everything together. You will also need a closed container for used bags. These can be emptied, rinsed and sealed in a plastic bag before being put in the dustbin, though in some fortunate areas the council makes special arrangements to collect this sort of rubbish.

You may be advised to take a special low-residue bland diet immediately after the operation, but should soon be able to return to eating normally. You may find that one or two foods upset you and you prefer to avoid them. If you develop constipation or diarrhoea, small changes in diet may help. More fluids, fruit and vegetables help to relieve constipation and a return to the low-residue diet should control diarrhoea. If this does not rapidly improve the situation, you should consult your doctor or stoma care nurse before taking any medicines.

Make sure any new doctor you encounter knows about your stoma, as its presence may alter your treatment for other conditions.

GALL BLADDER DISEASE

The gall bladder is a muscular bag which concentrates bile made by the liver before it enters the gut to help in the digestion of fats. Bile may solidify to form gallstones. If a gallstone gets stuck in the bile passages, it causes severe abdominal pain and vomiting. Jaundice (a yellow colour of the skin) occurs if the bile is unable to drain into the bowel, and occasionally infection can spread upwards to the liver. A painful inflammation of the stone-filled gall bladder itself also occurs. This is called cholecystitis. Despite the possibility of all these complications, it seems that many people with gallstones have no symptoms at all.

How your doctor can help If he thinks you have gallstones he is likely to refer you to the hospital for tests. These may involve x-ray studies of gall bladder function or an ultrasound examination. If gallstones are found you will probably be advised to have an operation, though in a few cases the stones can be dissolved by oral drugs. New techniques are being developed to break up gallstones within the body and thus avoid the need for surgery, but these procedures are still experimental.

If you have cholecystitis you will be admitted to hospital and given pain relief and antibiotics. Your gall bladder will be removed later when the infection has subsided. Jaundice due to a stuck gallstone is also treated surgically.

Helping yourself Your gall bladder symptoms are likely to become less troublesome if you eat a low-fat, high-fibre diet and lose weight.

The urinary system and genitals

The urinary apparatus consists of the kidneys, which manufacture urine, and their drainage system. It includes the ureters, which carry urine from the kidneys to the bladder, the urethra, which runs from the bladder to the outside world, and various nearby glands. In men the genitals consist of the testes that produce sperm, the glands that add ingredients to the semen and the ducts it passes through. The penis and the part of the urethra that lies within it is part of both systems. At different times urine is passed through it and semen is ejaculated along it during orgasm.

In women the urinary apparatus is similar, except that the urethra is much shorter and carries only urine. The female reproductive apparatus consists of the ovaries, the uterus and its Fallopian tubes and the vagina. The two systems are often considered together as the genitourinary system because their parts are adjacent and share some functions.

Common problems

PROSTATIC ENLARGEMENT

The prostate gland is found only in men. Its function is to contribute secretions to the semen. The prostate is about the size and shape of a chestnut and lies at the base of the bladder. Part of the urethra runs through it, carrying urine from the bladder to the penis for urination.

The prostate tends to enlarge as its owner gets older, and this interferes with urinary function. If you have an enlarged prostate you will notice that it is difficult to start to urinate. Your urinary stream will be slow and poor, and peters out into a dribble. You will find you need to visit the lavatory more often and to avoid accidents must do so without delay. Your sleep is likely to be disturbed by the need to pass urine during the night. If you are very unlucky you may find it difficult to control your urine and become slightly incontinent. A few sufferers suddenly become painfully unable to pass water at all and need urgent treatment for acute retention.

How your doctor can help On hearing your story he will examine your prostate gland with his gloved finger placed in your back passage. If it is enlarged he will refer you to the surgical clinic at the hospital. The usual operation is done with an instrument passed up the urethra, which can cut away the overgrown gland. This is called a transurethral resection or TUR. It can be done under a spinal anaesthetic, which abolishes pain but leaves the patient awake. A few patients need to have an open operation through an incision low down on the abdominal wall, and a general anaesthetic is needed for this. After either sort of surgery a catheter is left in place for a few days to drain urine from the bladder into a bag. This is removed once the raw area has stopped bleeding and urine can be passed normally again.

The doctor may prescribe medicine to relieve symptoms until the operation can be performed.

Sexual function may be altered after prostatectomy. After the TUR semen will be ejaculated backwards into the bladder rather than forwards through the penis. The orgasm will feel different to both partners, and the next lot of urine the man passes will be cloudy because of the semen it contains. 'Retrograde ejaculation' as this is called, does not interfere with general health or sexual enjoyment. The larger open operation causes impotence in a minority of patients. If you need a prostatectomy, you should make a point of discussing the likely effect on your sex life with the surgeon beforehand.

Helping yourself While waiting for a prostate operation, the frequent need to pass water is likely to be your worst problem. Resist the temptation to drink less so as to avoid the need to visit the lavatory: the dehydration this causes can damage your kidneys. If necessary, take all your fluids in the daytime with the last drink mid-evening so that your nights are as undisturbed as possible.

PROLAPSE

This condition affects the womb and vagina and of course only occurs in women. The normal supports of the womb are stretched during childbirth and the supporting ligaments weaken further after the menopause. A chronic cough or straining due to constipation makes a prolapse worse.

If you have a prolapse you may be troubled by an uncomfortable feeling of 'something coming down' between your legs. You may also have trouble controlling your urine, with a tendency to wet yourself slightly on coughing or picking up heavy shopping. Accidents may be especially likely if your bladder is full.

How your doctor can help Do not delay consulting him because of embarrassment. Your story will be familiar to him and he will be glad to help. Treatment depends on the nature and severity of the prolapse. Milder cases may get better with simple exercises to tone up the pelvic floor muscles, and a physiotherapist can teach you how to do them. Moderately severe prolapses can be controlled by a rubber ring pessary, which rests against the pelvic bones and holds the vagina and uterus in place. Alternatively, an operation can be performed to stitch the slipped tissues back into place, and your doctor may refer you to the hospital for this. The hospital doctor may need to order tests to show the workings of your bladder to help him decide which sort of operation will help you most. After the operation, you will be told to avoid heavy lifting and to postpone intercourse until the tissues are healed.

Helping yourself You can find out for yourself how to do pelvic floor exercises by writing to the continence adviser at the Disabled Living Foundation. Persevering with these may be sufficient to relieve symptoms in milder cases. Pant liners or mini-pads may also provide a feeling of security. To avoid accidents, you may decide to restrict fluids before a journey, but be sure to make up for it later in the day, as dehydration can be dangerous. Do not be too shy to ask for help if your prolapse is starting to interfere with your normal active life.

The nervous system

The brain, the spinal cord running down from it within the backbone and the network of nerves carrying information throughout the body make up the nervous system. It is responsible for communications inside the body, and it also processes information reaching it from the outside world via the senses. It compares this with the knowledge stored in the memory and then organizes the body's response.

Common problems

STROKE

A stroke is called a cerebrovascular accident (CVA) by doctors. It happens when a brain blood vessel becomes blocked, either suddenly (cerebral embolus) or gradually (cerebral thrombosis). Strokes also happen when brain blood vessels burst (cerebral haemorrhage). Bleeding is much less common than blockage, but the effects on the sufferer are very similar.

If the blockage is complete, the part of the brain supplied by the damaged blood vessel dies and the part of the body it controls loses its function. The sufferer may vomit or become confused, and in more severe cases can slip gradually or suddenly into unconsciousness. When the doctor is called, he will find evidence of the damage to the brain. Most commonly there is loss of feeling and of the ability to move down one side of the body. The medical name for this is hemiparesis, meaning 'half-paralysis'. The stroke patient may also lose his ability to speak intelligibly or to understand what others are saying. Part of his field of vision may be lost, and he may also lose control of his urine.

In a major or completed stroke these symptoms persist for more than twenty-four hours. When a similar pattern of illness occurs but passes off within that time, the patient is said to have had a transient ischaemic attack or TIA. TIAs happen when a vessel blockage clears itself spontaneously. They should be reported to the doctor as prompt medical treatment can prevent the later development of a full-blown stroke.

How your doctor can help He should call without delay to make certain of the diagnosis and to decide together with you and your family whether home or hospital care will be best. If there is no one able to look after you at home – and heavy nursing duties may be involved – then a transfer to hospital may be necessary. There may also be medical reasons to prefer hospital care. First, tests may be necessary to find out whether there is something to put right to prevent another stroke. Second, how well a patient recovers from a stroke depends on the severity of the brain damage and also very largely on the quality of his rehabilitation. If physiotherapists, occupational therapists and speech therapists are only available in a hospital setting, it may be better for you to go into hospital even if you would much prefer to stay at home.

In the early stages of your stroke illness, you will need adequate fluids and nourishment, correct positioning of your paralysed limbs and regular turning to prevent complications such as bed sores. Once the acute stage is passed, the emphasis changes to rehabilitation, so that despite your stroke you will be able to enjoy as independent a life as possible.

Helping yourself A stroke is a shattering experience, and you will inevitably be very distressed if you cannot do much for yourself for a while afterwards. Mourning your loss of independence is quite natural, but as with other sorts of grieving, it tends to improve as time passes. Discuss with your doctors the likelihood of a second stroke. A recurrence can often be prevented by medicines to control blood pressure or by changes in lifestyle such as losing weight or stopping smoking.

Try to cooperate with rehabilitation as far as possible. It is normal to become exasperated from time to time. You will need someone to tell about your feelings who will not be surprised or upset by normal human anger and bad temper. A Stroke Club may be helpful.

Carers of stroke patients also have their difficulties. If you are one, Chapter 4 may be of help. While the stroke sufferer is in hospital, you should keep in contact with the staff who are caring for him and helping him to regain his independence. A home visit will usually be made to find out what aids and adaptations will be needed to help you both manage at home. Usually the stroke victim will come home for a short period such as a weekend to iron out any small problems before his final discharge. You should find out how much your relative can do for himself and where he needs unobtrusive help, as this will help you to preserve his independence and self-respect as far as possible.

If your relative has a speech problem, try to ensure he is seen by a speech therapist, who will be able to give you guidance as to how you and others around him can help him regain his speech.

The Chest, Heart and Stroke Association can provide helpful information about all aspects of caring for a stroke victim. It also runs Stroke Clubs and relatives' groups in many areas, and these provide mutual support as well as social contact. You would be well advised to get in touch with the Association if you have suffered a stroke or live with a stroke victim. See page 168.

PARKINSON'S DISEASE
This affects the ability to move, and the early stages are often difficult to recognize. Typically, tasks such as dressing and washing take longer, and patterns of coordinated movement become awkward – for instance, that needed for getting out of a car. Repetitive tasks such as polishing or stirring a saucepan become difficult and handwriting becomes awkward, smaller and less legible. Younger patients may develop a tremor, but this is rarer in older ones who may have painful muscle rigidity. The movement difficulty affects the facial muscles, so the expression alters less with changes of mood. The face becomes rather mask-like and it may be difficult to stop saliva drooling from the corners of the mouth. Speech may become quieter and a little slurred. Walking becomes difficult and shuffling, and a hunched posture is usually adopted. All these symptoms are common, but they do not all occur in any one patient. They may be worse on some days than on others, and it is important to remember that this is part of the disease and does not happen because the sufferer

is 'not trying'. Though depression may require treatment the mental faculties are usually unimpaired except occasionally in the late stages of the illness.

Parkinson's Disease happens because parts of the brain are lacking in the substance dopamine. This is a neurotransmitter, that is, a chemical by which the brain does its work. Why this lack occurs is usually not known; Parkinson's does not seem to run in families. A few cases follow the use of drugs called phenothia-zines to treat severe mental illness.

Patients with Parkinson's do tend to get worse as time passes, but with modern drugs and other methods of treatment the outlook is better than it was even a few years ago, and advances in treatment continue to be made. The vast majority of sufferers have a manageable level of disability and can look forward to many years of independence and a normal life-span.

How your doctor can help If he thinks you have Parkinson's, your GP is likely to refer you to the appropriate hospital specialist, a neurologist. This is because an extensive experience of the diagnosis and management of Parkinson's is necessary if you are to have correctly prescribed medication tailored to your needs. The neurologist may also suggest physiotherapy or speech ther-apy, and an occupational therapist's advice may be useful in recommending home aids and adaptations to help you with the tasks of daily living.

Helping yourself Modern drugs are powerful and it is very important that for maximum benefit in the long term you take them exactly as prescribed (see pages 119–21).

Try to keep as active as you can, continuing with your daily round if at all possible. A slower pace of work may help, as may mechanical equipment such as a typewriter. Your doctor or the physiotherapist will probably suggest special exercises adapted to your condition to help you cope with the disease, and you should do these when you can without becoming overtired. Try not to withdraw from society or to let your family do everything for you out of misplaced kindness. Though often difficult and slow, it does seem that the more you do the more you will remain able to do.

If you drive you must notify the Department of Transport at Swansea that you have been diagnosed as suffering from Parkinson's Disease. The Department will then ask your doctors for a report on your health. It may be safe for patients with mild symptoms to drive, but in more severe cases it may be necessary for them to stop.

You would be well advised to get in touch with the Parkinson's Disease Society (see page 169). Apart from funding research, the Society produces helpful literature and has local branches which organize social events and fund-raising.

DEPRESSION

Everyone feels sad from time to time. It would be inhuman not to mourn the loss of a loved one or to be discouraged by a disabling illness. Depression as an illness is an exaggerated caricature of 'normal' misery. Psychiatrists call it depressive disorder. People with depressive disorder are obviously sad, usually feeling at their worst in the morning and improving slightly as the day wears on. They become inactive and apathetic, abandoning their usual interests and hobbies and neglecting personal appearance and hygiene. They may be agitated and constantly on the move, though to little purpose. Sleep tends to be disturbed by early morning waking, when the sufferers worry over their failures and inadequacies. Appetite and weight are lost, constipation develops and sufferers may complain of distressing and inexplicable physical symptoms such as headache, backache and abdominal distress. In severe cases patients experience overwhelming guilt over imagined or minor faults, and may blame themselves for large-scale catastrophes such as wars. Depressive disorder is never trivial and can be fatal – either because of extreme self-neglect or as the result of suicide.

Some elderly people with depressive disorder have a bipolar type of illness, with episodes in which they are restless, excitable and aggressive. During these they may wrongly believe themselves to be very rich or to have made great sexual conquests. Their behaviour under these delusions may not only embarrass relatives, but also lead to serious consequences. Fortunately this type of depression is also treatable, with lithium (see page 121).

Close families usually notice the change in personality and behaviour when a member develops depressive disorder. In an old people's home, however, the condition may be more difficult to spot. Withdrawn and passive behaviour, a hypochondriacal preoccupation with health, a clinging need for reassurance or aggressive non-cooperation may be thought of as 'just old age' or 'second childhood'. In fact, these symptoms may be signs of a depressive disorder which will respond to treatment.

'Ageist' attitudes may also lead to depressive disorder going unnoticed, as people who think – wrongly – that being old must be a depressing experience will not regard misery and desperation as abnormal.

Who gets depressive disorder? No type of person is immune. It does often seem to follow a loss or an accumulation of losses, a sequences of events which is quite common in later life. People may mourn a lost partner or friends, home or the end of a fulfilling career, and after feeling low for a while, slowly return to a tolerably comfortable way of life. Others may respond to loss by developing a depressive disorder. This is especially likely to happen if mental resilience is reduced by illness or disability or by poor social circumstances; the lack of a close confiding relationship seems to be particularly lowering to the spirits. None the less, some cases of depressive disorder happen out of the blue.

How your doctor can help Suicidal impulses must always be taken seriously as they are sometimes acted upon. If you feel tempted to end your life or if a friend confides this to you, it is important that the doctor is consulted without delay. In less severe cases medical help should be sought if sadness is interfering with normal life or if low spirits persist longer after a loss than they would be expected to. Depressive disorder paralyses the will. People with severe depression will lack the motivation to ask for help, and will only get the aid they need if their relatives and friends organize it for them.

Sometimes the family doctor will feel able to care for the de-pressed person himself, but in more severe cases he will seek referral to a psychiatrist. He or she is a medically qualified doctor who will have had special training in mental illness and its treatment.

Two sorts of treatment are available; the psychological or 'talking' therapies, such as the various sorts of psychotherapy, and the 'medical' treatments such as tablets and ECT. The two sorts are not mutually exclusive, and many patients have both. In general, less severely ill people benefit from psychological treat-ment and do not need medical intervention, while sicker ones will be unable to participate in psychological treatment until they have recovered a little in response to medical measures. Details of medicines used for depressive disorder will be found in Chapter 3.

Patients with severe depressive disorder may be admitted to hospital for their own safety. Some of these are helped by electrical treatment (ECT) which is given under anaesthesia.

Helping yourself If you are severely depressed you cannot help yourself. It is as silly and unkind to tell depressed people to 'pull themselves together' as to expect an accident victim to walk on a broken leg. However, in milder cases or in severe ones once the worse of the illness is over, there is a lot that people getting over depressive disorder can do to help themselves – see 'Avoiding Depression' in the previous chapter. In particular, there is some evidence that feeling powerless to influence one's circumstances is a potent cause of depression. It makes sense to take charge of one's own life as far as possible.

Sadly, some people still regard mental illness such as depressive disorder as a shameful sign of weakness. There are no grounds for this idea; depressive disorder commonly attacks conscientious people who achieve great things between black times; Winston Churchill and Sigmund Freud are outstanding examples. No one should ever feel ashamed of the misfortune of an illness, whether mental or physical.

SHINGLES

This is really localized chicken pox and is caused by the same herpes zoster virus. It is believed that after the original attack the virus lies dormant in the nerves until it is reactivated and causes an attack of shingles. Why this happens is usually not known. The site of the condition shows which nerves are affected. The affected area feels tender and painful for a few days before the rash appears. Redness of the skin is followed by blisters like drops of water which dry to form a scab. The patient may feel feverish and generally unwell.

Shingles most commonly affects one side of the trunk, but an especially unpleasant site is the forehead and eye (ophthalmic herpes).

How your doctor can help He can identify the disease and prescribe treatment (see page 122). Patients with ophthalmic herpes and those with severe disease elsewhere may need admission to hospital.

Helping yourself Follow your doctor's advice about medication carefully. Remember you are infectious until the scabs have crusted, and can transmit chicken pox, especially to someone in intimate contact, for example helping with personal care. Pregnant women are at risk of developing a severe form and having a miscarriage. It is not known whether shingles itself can be transmitted in this way.

A few people have persistent pain after an attack of shingles. If you are unlucky enough to experience this 'post-herpetic neuralgia' you should ask your doctor to refer you to a pain clinic for expert help.

The eyes

Light enters the front of the eye through a transparent window, the cornea. The light is then focussed on to the retina at the back of the eye by the cornea, the lens and the fluids within the eye. The retina is sensitive to light and impulses are sent from it along the optic nerve to the brain. Here they are interpreted and compared with memory stores.

As middle age advances, most people find they need to hold small print further away from their eyes in order to see it clearly. This is due to ageing changes in the lens and reading glasses usually put things right. Otherwise sight should not change with age, and any deterioration in vision should be promptly reported to the optician or doctor.

Common problems

CATARACT

This is due to changes in the protein that makes up the lens of the eye. The lens gradually becomes opaque and white instead of clear and transparent. This causes clouding of vision which is especially noticeable in a bright light, and the sight gradually worsens as more of the lens changes.

How your doctor can help By examining your eyes through an instrument called an ophthalmoscope he can establish that you have cataracts. An opthalmoscope is a modified torch with an assortment of magnifying lenses through which the inside of the eyeball can be examined. Cataracts are commonly present in both eyes, but usually one is worse than the other. For treatment you will need to see an ophthalmic surgeon at the hospital, as the only remedy is to remove the lens. This is usually done when vision has become bad enough to interfere with reading and other activities. After the operation the lost focussing power of the eye has to be replaced by an artificial lens. This can be positioned in front of the eye in spectacles, on the eyeball as a contact lens, or within the eyeball as a lens implant. Which is used depends on individual circumstances. Although techniques are improving all the time, no substitute is as good as the natural lens of the eye, so the cataract operation is not performed until the natural lens has become too opaque to be useful.

Helping yourself Before the operation you will see best through your cloudy lens if you are not dazzled. Tinted spectacles (the lightest tint that is comfortable) will help, and so will a hat with a brim or a peaked cap. At home, good lighting with diffusing shades will be useful in making the most of remaining sight. Door handles and edges can be highlighted with coloured tape and light food put on a dark plate or vice versa. Low vision aids such as magnifiers can be obtained through the hospital eye service and other useful articles from the RNIB (see page 170) or Partially Sighted Society (see page 169).

After the operation you are likely to be out of bed the following day. Once home you should follow advice to avoid heavy lifting and forward bending. Be especially careful to close all cupboard doors, or you may bang your head.

If you are given a lens implant, your sight will be better almost immediately after the operation and within a few weeks you should be back to normal life. Things will take a little longer with the other alternatives. Contact lens users need a certain amount of manual dexterity, but the lenses become easier to manage with practice. Cataract spectacles have a magnifying effect, making it difficult to judge distances at first. You have to look straight through the centre of the lens to see properly, so it is necessary to turn your head to see objects near the edge of your field of vision. Persevering wearers who use their cataract spectacles for increasing times each day find they rapidly get used to them.

You will find further information in Age Concern's book, *In Touch with Cataracts*.

GLAUCOMA

Glaucoma happens when the pressure of the fluids inside the eye rises. The fragile light-sensitive retina lining the back of the eye is damaged and cannot repair itself. Acute glaucoma produces very poor vision in the affected eye, which looks red and is very painful. The patient feels very unwell and sick and may vomit. The chronic form of glaucoma is more common and causes a gradual loss of vision which may not be noticed by the patient.

Every year people become blind because of glaucoma, and prompt treatment could prevent this happening.

How your doctor can help Your family doctor will usually send you to the eye clinic of the local hospital for the diagnosis to be confirmed and treatment to be organized. Acute cases often require surgery. Laser treatment can often be used instead of a conventional operation, and this causes much less upset. Less severe cases are treated with tablets, eyedrops or both.

Helping yourself Be sure to have your sight tested at least every two years, and more often if you notice any problems. If anyone in your family suffers from glaucoma you should tell your optician, as you will be slightly more likely to develop it yourself. He will be able to measure the pressure inside your eyeball with a special machine. This is neither painful nor time-consuming and could save your sight.

DIABETIC RETINOPATHY

Retinopathy means retinal disease. New blood vessels grow into the retinae of some diabetics' eyes and can pose a threat to sight. The vessels can bleed into the fluid within the eye and the clot can pull the retina off as it shrinks during healing (retinal detachment).

How your doctor can help The changes of diabetic retinopathy can be clearly seen on examining the eye with an ophthalmoscope. Your doctor can ensure that you and all his other diabetic patients have regular eye checks. If necessary, new blood vessels can be painlessly clotted and rendered harmless using a laser beam, without the need for open surgery.

Helping yourself However stable your diabetes, you should make sure you attend for your eye checks at the intervals suggested by your doctor or clinic (usually every six months to one year). Depending on local circumstances, the examinations may be performed at your doctor's surgery, the hospital or your optician's consulting room.

Eye complications seem to be less common in people with well-controlled diabetes, so it is wise to keep to your treatment plan.

MACULAR DEGENERATION
The macula is the centre of the visual field and is affected more than the edges in this condition. The sufferer notices that shapes look distorted – for instance, the edges of doors appear curved rather than straight.

How your doctor can help Unfortunately macular degeneration cannot be cured, though laser treatment can halt its progress in a few cases. Your GP may send you to the eye clinic to make sure the diagnosis is correct and any necessary treatment is given.

Helping yourself Because the edges of the visual field are largely spared by macular degeneration, you are likely to find it easier to get about and care for yourself than some other visually handicapped people. However, your reading vision is likely to be poor: information about Braille or Moon and Talking Books is available from the RNIB or Partially Sighted Society.

RETINAL DETACHMENT
The retina is as soft and fragile as the skin on hot milk. It can be stripped off the inside of the eyeball by the force of a blow or by the healing process after a retinal vessel has bled.

Retinal detachment produces typical symptoms: the affected person says that part of his visual field has gone black, as if a curtain had been drawn or a shutter descended. Without treatment this can cause partial or complete blindness, but prompt treatment can minimize the damage. A laser beam is used to stick down the edges of the tear and thus preserve remaining sight.

How your doctor can help He can send you to an eye hospital for treatment without delay.

Helping yourself If you suffer a sudden loss of vision you should seek medical help at once, either from your GP or the casualty department of an eye hospital.

CONJUNCTIVITIS

The conjunctiva is the thin membrane that lines the eyelids and covers the part of the eyeball exposed between them when the lids are open. When the conjunctiva becomes infected, the eye feels gritty and uncomfortable. The blood vessels in the white of the eye are dilated, giving the condition its common name of 'pink eye'. Pus may stick the eyelids together during sleep and collect at the corner of the eye during the day.

How your doctor can help He can prescribe an antibiotic as an ointment or drops. Conjunctivitis usually gets better very quickly when treated.

Helping yourself While conjunctivitis is not serious, a pink eye can occasionally result from much rarer conditions that threaten sight. It is sensible to see your doctor urgently if you have a red, sore or painful eye.

Do not bathe your eye unless your doctor tells you to. You may find cotton wool soaked in warm water useful for removing dried secretions from eyelids and lashes.

GIANT CELL ARTERITIS

In this condition (also called temporal arteritis) the arteries supplying the face, scalp and eye become inflamed and partially blocked by the big cells that give the condition its name. Sufferers, usually elderly women, feel generally unwell and complain of pain on one or both sides of the head. It may hurt to chew food, and the scalp and face may be tender to touch. If the eye arteries are involved, sight can be affected, and once the sufferer notices visual disturbances she needs treatment without further delay.

People with giant cell arteritis are more likely than others to suffer from polymyalgia rheumatica (see page 80).

How your doctor can help Steroid therapy needs to be started as soon as possible (see pages 131–2). Beginning this is quite a serious decision, so the diagnosis needs to be certain. It is made by clinical examination, a blood test and a biopsy of the temporal artery. This involves a small operation to take a small piece of tissue from the temple so it can be examined under a microscope. Your doctor will organize this so that as little time as possible is wasted. Once the steroids have controlled the condition, the dose can be reduced and the tablets often withdrawn altogether after a year or so, without risk to sight.

Helping yourself Sudden disturbances of vision always need urgent medical attention, and you should make sure you get this.

The ears

The shell-like ear flap leads into the outer ear canal which conducts sound-waves inwards to the ear drum. On the other side of the drum are three tiny, jointed bones which carry the sound-waves across the air-filled middle ear cavity to the inner ear. Here the hearing organ transforms sound vibrations into electrical impulses. These then run along the auditory nerve to the brain, where they are interpreted and compared with past experiences. The inner ear is also concerned with balance, so inner ear disease can cause unsteadiness as well as hearing problems.

Common problems

DEAFNESS

As the years pass, many people lose some of their earlier ability to hear high-pitched sounds. Distorted speech, such as train announcements in railway stations, may become more difficult to understand. It may also become harder to understand a single speaker in a noisy public place. However, if you start to find it difficult to join in group conversation, cannot hear the telephone or doorbell, or need the TV or radio turned up too loud for the comfort of other people, you are suffering from abnormal hearing loss (deafness). Medically speaking this can be 'conductive' or 'perceptive' – also called sensorineural or nerve deafness.

Conductive deafness happens when something interferes with the passage of sound through the outer or middle ear. Wax in the ear canal is a common and easily remedied cause. Perforated ear drums also interfere with hearing. In some elderly people the drum may have been burst by an ear infection, often long ago in childhood, while in others it was ruptured by the wartime blast of a nearby gun or bomb. Blast can also damage the tiny middle ear bones, which can also be affected by the disease otosclerosis. This starts in middle age, and freezes one of the bones into its tiny socket so the chain can no longer transmit vibration to the inner ear. Many causes of conductive deafness are curable.

Perceptive or nerve deafness is due to disease of or damage to the inner ear or the auditory nerve connecting it to the brain. Nerve tissue cannot heal itself, so this sort of deafness cannot usually be cured. However, careful management can still make life much more enjoyable for the deaf person.

Presbyacusis is the name given to the type of nerve deafness common in elderly people. High-pitched sounds such as t's and s's become difficult to hear, so speech is distorted. 'Loudness recruitment' means that a slight increase in the loudness of a sound becomes painfully intense to the hearer. This can happen when someone merely raises their voice slightly. The deafness may be worse on some days than on others and may be accompanied by tinnitus (see below).

Ménière's Disease starts in middle age with attacks of giddiness, sickness and impaired hearing. The attacks gradually cease but nerve deafness persists into old age. Inner ear deafness and damage can also follow some sorts of drug treatment, a head injury, exposure to blast, or a noisy occupation.

How your doctor can help He will examine your ears with an auriscope, an instrument which shines a light down a detachable funnel. The ear canal and ear drum can then be inspected through magnifying lenses. Your doctor may be able to identify an obvious problem, or he may find his view blocked by large quantities of wax, which he will remove. If you are still deaf after this, he will refer you to the hearing clinic at the local hospital, where the cause and pattern of your deafness will be identified and appropriate treatment can be arranged. Once your hearing is as good as treatment can make it, you may be offered a hearing aid.

Helping yourself Do not accept deafness as 'just old age', as treatment can often help a great deal. You may need to insist that your difficulty is properly investigated and identified.

TINNITUS

The tinnitus sufferer is bothered by 'noises in the ear' which tend to be especially troublesome at night. They are usually due to inner ear malfunction and are very rarely a sign of illness. Aspirin in large quantities occasionally causes tinnitus which gets better once the drug is stopped.

How your doctor can help He can first make sure your ears are free from wax and that you are not taking any drugs that might cause tinnitus. He may then decide to refer you to an ENT (ear, nose and throat) surgeon; a list of consultants at centres specializing in tinnitus is available from the British Tinnitus Association (see page 170). Having examined you, the ENT specialist will almost certainly be able to reassure you that nothing is seriously wrong and that your tinnitus is unlikely to become worse. Once your mind has been put at rest in this way, you may find you are able to ignore the noise, just as you would that of a familiar ticking clock. However, if your symptoms persist, other things can be done. A few people are helped by drug treatment, while the most effective treatment is the tinnitus 'masker'. This is a device which fits in the ear like a hearing aid. It produces a noise which conceals that of the tinnitus and usually has a soothing effect of its own. A masker must be fitted by an expert, and is unfortunately not nationally available under the NHS.

Helping yourself You will probably want to get in touch with the British Tinnitus Association. This provides information, funds research and also runs a number of self-help groups around the country.

In addition to the treatments outlined above, some tinnitus

sufferers report benefit from activities that reduce stress, such as yoga and relaxation techniques (see page 28).

Should you require a mild painkiller, paracetamol is less likely to aggravate your tinnitus than a preparation containing aspirin.

The blood

Blood is the body's transport system and an important means of distributing heat around it. It carries oxygen and nutrients to wherever they are needed for body growth and repair and takes waste products to the kidneys to be disposed of in the urine. Chemicals such as hormones produced within the body or drugs introduced from outside also travel in the blood.

Common problems

ANAEMIA

This happens when the blood contains less than normal of the red pigment called haemoglobin which carries oxygen round the body. A common cause is leakage of blood from the gut. This may be due to a comparatively trivial condition such as piles, or more seriously, to a hiatus hernia, peptic ulcer or diverticular disease. Occasionally the cause is a bleeding bowel cancer. Some drugs used to treat arthritis can also irritate the gut lining and cause oozing of blood.

Anaemia can also result from a lack of nutrients, either when the diet is poor in iron and vitamins or when bowel disease prevents the proper absorption of foodstuffs. Pernicious anaemia is the type caused by difficulty in absorbing Vitamin B_{12} and is serious if not treated. As well as the usual symptoms of anaemia the sufferer may have signs of nerve damage such as tingling in the limbs, loss of sensation in the feet and occasionally mental confusion.

Anaemia may be quite difficult to detect. Pallor is common, but many people have fair skins and normal blood. Anaemic people may have sore mouths and tongues and also complain of dizziness, tiredness and shortness of breath. Sometimes they become apathetic, neglecting themselves and their homes and becoming increasingly likely to fall. Once in this state they are unlikely to seek help for themselves, but need someone else to notice that they are less well than they were.

How your doctor can help He can find out whether or not you are anaemic by sending a sample of your blood to the laboratory for testing. These tests will also help to find the cause of the anaemia. If you have bleeding from the bowel, he will also organize tests to find the cause of this. When all the test results are available treatment can be arranged. Underlying causes of blood loss or poor food absorption may need hospital treatment to correct them. Alternatively, poor eating habits may need to be put right and prescribed medicines may be necessary to replace missing iron or vitamins. People with pernicious anaemia will need vitamin B_{12} injections every three months for the rest of their lives, but provided they get these, can remain perfectly healthy.

Helping yourself If you vomit blood or pass a black, tarry motion you need urgent treatment. Smaller quantities of blood in the stool are usually due to easily corrected minor abnormalities. However, if you are unlucky enough to have a bowel cancer, early treatment can produce a complete cure, so avoid delay in diagnosis by seeing your doctor promptly.

A good diet need be neither expensive nor time-consuming to prepare. See Chapter 1 for further guidelines on healthy eating.

If you are taking tablets for arthritis, you should report any symptoms of indigestion or abdominal pain to your doctor. If you have to wait a day or so to see him, stop taking the tablets in the meantime.

The bones, joints and muscles

Bones consist of a protein scaffolding stiffened with calcium. They meet and move on each other at the joints, where the bone ends are covered in shiny cartilage, enclosed in a capsule and lubricated with fluid. The muscles make up the 'flesh' of the body. They run between bones and shorten to produce movement at joints.

Common problems

OSTEOPOROSIS

In this condition the bones become less substantial and more fragile with increasing age. It is far commoner in women (once the menopause is past) than in men. Its most dangerous consequence is that the bones break easily after trivial injury. Sufferers also complain of back pain, probably due to squashing of a vertebra.

How your doctor can help It is generally thought that hormone replacement therapy (HRT) helps to prevent bone loss in women. Other treatment can be used in women who cannot take HRT though this is unfortunately less effective (see pages 126–7). Men do not require hormone replacement of this sort.

For a squashed vertebra, the usual treatment is a short period of rest followed by mobilization, with drugs for pain. A back-support may help the patient to keep comfortable, and fluoride tablets may prevent a recurrence.

Helping yourself Taking exercise helps to keep bones strong. Also, the improvement in muscle strength and coordination helps to make a fall less likely.

Adequate calcium and Vitamin D help to strengthen bones if taken with HRT; they probably have little effect without. Your diet should include half a pint of milk a day, half a pound of cheese a week and oily fish such as mackerel, sardines or pilchards once a week. Low-fat milk and cheese contain just as much calcium as full-fat. Excess alcohol and smoking seem to make osteoporosis worse – yet another reason for adopting a healthy lifestyle.

BROKEN BONES (FRACTURES)

A broken hip (femur) is a very common injury in older women. Some cases are due to simple accident such as tripping on an uneven paving stone, and the patient is usually quickly back on her feet. In people over eighty the fall is often the result of an illness rather than of tripping, and in these cases recovery is less certain.

Colles' fracture of the wrist is also common. This usually happens when somebody who is falling tries to save herself and takes the full impact on her outstretched hand.

How your doctor can help Old bones heal well if their owner is properly looked after, and no time is lost. If you break your hip you should expect to be operated on within twenty-four hours. Usually the broken-off top of your hip-bone will be replaced by an artificial part. This will enable you to get back on your feet quickly, and you may expect to take a few steps with help the day after the operation. The geriatric–orthopaedic team of therapists, doctors and nurses will help you to get back to your normal level of activity, and if all goes well you should leave the hospital about five weeks after your admission.

A Colles' fracture is usually 'reduced' under anaesthetic (that is, the bones are put back into their proper position). They are then held still by a plaster cast so as to heal correctly.

Helping yourself Many falls can be prevented by removing trip hazards from the home and being sensibly careful about activities like replacing light bulbs and reaching high shelves (see Chapter 1). After a fractured hip, cooperating with rehabilitation is very important if you are to return to independent living. Activity is also important after a Colles' fracture. To get back to normal quickly, it is wise to follow the advice of your doctors and therapists in using the damaged arm. In the early stages this will help to disperse swelling, while later on it will help to restore the arm to its normal function. A heat pad on the arm and the sensible use of painkillers will help with this.

PAGET'S DISEASE
This is a condition of bone overgrowth. Its cause is unknown. About half of all sufferers experience little trouble from their

Paget's, which may be discovered only by chance. The unlucky 50 per cent of patients have pain, and their enlarging bones may change in shape. Their legs may become bowed and the top of their heads enlarge so that hats no longer fit. The facial appearance is however not affected. Sometimes the overgrown bone can press on nerves, causing pain and disability, while deafness can occur if the nerve from the ear is squashed. Short-circuiting of blood through newly grown bone sometimes worsens heart failure.

How your doctor can help He can establish that you do in fact have Paget's Disease. His examination, plus a combination of blood and urine tests and x-rays, will usually make sure of the diagnosis and he may call on help from his hospital colleagues. After this he can advise you as to whether treatment is necessary and if so, what sort. Many people with Paget's Disease require no treatment at all, or at most mild pain-killers. Others need treatment to suppress bone activity (see page 127).

Helping yourself It is sensible to report back to your doctor at once if your pain becomes worse. This usually only indicates a flare-up of the disease, which can be controlled by treatment. Sometimes such pain is due to a bone having broken through an area of disordered growth, and surgical treatment may be necessary to help it heal. Very occasionally, swelling and pain happen because a tumour has developed, and this requires prompt treatment.

OSTEOARTHRITIS

Arthritis means joint inflammation. The commonest form of this is osteoarthritis, also called osteoarthrosis (OA). It is uncomfortable and a nuisance, but rarely causes crippling and does not shorten life.

OA may be due to the effects of constant wear and tear on a joint, aggravated by any injury the joint has suffered. Overweight may worsen the disease in the weight-bearing joints, the hips, knees and spine. Women seem particularly prone to OA in their hands. These then get gnarled-looking around the finger joints and may become squared-off in shape if the joint at the base of the thumb is affected.

If you have OA, your most likely complaints will be of pain and stiffness, often worse in the mornings or following a change in the weather. Your daily living difficulties will depend on which of your joints are affected: for instance, it is difficult to do fine work with osteoarthritic hands, and osteoarthritic knees are particularly uncomfortable when walking downstairs.

How your doctor can help With an examination and perhaps tests he will make sure that it is OA and nothing more serious that is causing the trouble. If pain is your main problem, he will prescribe painkillers. It will help him to know what time of day the pain is worse so that he can tailor his treatment to your pain. Digestive diseases such as peptic ulcer may be made worse by some anti-arthritic drugs; if you have an ulcer you should remind your doctor of the fact.

If he thinks it will help, he may refer you to the physiotherapist. She will show you exercises which will strengthen your muscles and help joint movement. She may also suggest you use a walking stick to relieve the strain on a painful joint by taking some of the body's weight. A stick's height should correspond to yours: its length from the top of the handle to the tip should be the same as the distance from your wrist crease to the ground when you stand erect. Hold the stick in the hand *opposite* to the painful leg: this arrangement helps you to walk normally and reduces the chances of falling over. The physiotherapist will advise on stick materials (aluminium or wood) and the best shape of handle for your particular needs. She will also know where you can get replacement rubber ferrules; worn ones are liable to slip and cause falls.

Some patients with osteoarthritis eventually need joint replacement. This involves substituting an artificial metal or plastic joint for a natural but arthritic one – usually a hip or knee. No manufactured joint is as good as Nature's original model, but a replacement joint may be more mobile than an arthritic one and is of course pain-free. If you are considering a joint replacement, it is wise to discuss its merits and disadvantages carefully with the surgeon beforehand to make sure your hopes for improvement are likely to be fulfilled.

You may find the waiting list is long in your area. If so it may help to ask your family doctor if he can refer you elsewhere for earlier treatment.

Before the operation a careful assessment will be made by the team of people who will look after you following surgery. Doctors, nurses, physiotherapists, occupational therapists and social workers are likely to be involved. After the operation they will continue to make every effort to get you back on your feet and home again as soon as possible. If all goes well you may take a step between bed and chair on the day after the operation, and return home within two weeks. Things may take a little longer if your case is not quite straightforward.

After a number of years your artificial joint may itself need replacing because of wear and tear.

Helping yourself If you are overweight it will help to lose the excess and reduce the load your painful joints have to carry. Putting all your joints through their full range of movement daily is useful. You may find swimming in a heated pool or an exercise class for pensioners helpful. Avoid any exercise that hurts at the time you do it, as overworking a painful joint does more harm than good. Selective activity is best: arthritic knees may hurt when climbing stairs, but tolerate walking on flat ground well.

Many arthritis sufferers find that heat relieves discomfort and stiffness. A warm bath first thing may help to get you going, and an electrically-heated pad with a thermostatic control can be a useful purchase.

Tasks such as ironing may be more comfortable if done sitting down. If coping with chores is becoming difficult, you can get in touch with the community occupational therapist via your local Social Services Department. She can suggest and arrange for various aids and adaptations to your home to make things easier.

You may also like to see the range of available equipment at the Disabled Living Foundation or in your local chain-chemist.

The self-help organization for all arthritis sufferers is the Arthritis and Rheumatism Council (see page 167).

GOUT

This happens when crystals of a substance called monosodium urate form within a joint cavity and irritate its lining. This substance may also form hard, visible lumps called tophi on the ears, fingers or other sites in the body.

In the first attack a single joint, often the one at the base of the big toe, becomes acutely inflamed, red, shiny and very tender. On later occasions other joints may be affected, sometimes several at once.

How your doctor can help To confirm his diagnosis of gout he will organize blood tests and x-rays and possibly also the sampling of a small quantity of joint fluid to be examined under the microscope. A visit to or a short stay in hospital may be necessary.

Treatment in the acute stage is by tablets. Sometimes these need to be continued indefinitely to prevent a recurrence of the disease. Some diuretic drugs make gout worse, and these will be stopped if at all possible.

Helping yourself Gout is not necessarily a sign of high living! However, if you are overweight or drinking more than is good for you, adopting a healthier lifestyle may prevent further painful attacks.

'FROZEN SHOULDER'

This may happen in joints damaged by a fall or in those affected by a stroke, though careful attention to the position and movement of the arm during recovery should prevent it.

Inflammation in the tissues around the shoulder joint leads to pain and limitation of arm movement. Raising the arm may be particularly unpleasant, and dressing becomes awkward and uncomfortable. Sleep may be disturbed if the sufferer turns to lie on the frozen shoulder.

How your doctor can help He can order an x-ray of your painful shoulder to rule out more serious causes. Treatment usually involves steroid injections, heat or exercises in whatever combination is most useful for your condition.

Helping yourself Make sure you are involved in designing a treatment plan you can follow. You can afford to remain optimistic: most people's frozen shoulders get completely better within eighteen months, and the rest have only very slight continuing symptoms.

POLYMYALGIA RHEUMATICA (PMR)

This causes aching pain and stiffness in the muscles round the shoulders and sometimes also in the buttock and thigh muscles. Symptoms are worse in the morning or after a period of rest. Some people also feel generally unwell, have a mild fever and lose weight. PMR sufferers are more likely than other people to develop giant cell arteritis. Both conditions are commoner in women but the cause is unknown.

How your doctor can help Blood tests will usually establish the diagnosis; he may also suggest a biopsy of your temporal artery. Steroid therapy will be prescribed, and this will quickly make you feel better. PMR usually improves between six months and two years after it is diagnosed. Once improvement begins the steroids can be tailed off.

Helping yourself Steroids are powerful and sometimes life-saving drugs, but their unwanted effects are serious. It is sensible to make sure you understand how to use them by referring to the section on steroids in Chapter 3 (pages 131–2).

PAIN IN THE NECK

An acute stiff neck may occur after carrying a heavy suitcase or sleeping in an awkward position. If pain and a tingling sensation spread down the arm, the cause may be a slipped disc between the neck vertebrae. Pain in the neck extending up into the head may be due to osteoarthritis in the neck region of the spine.

How your doctor can help He can find out the cause of the trouble, using x-rays to supplement the results of his examination if he thinks this is necessary. He will prescribe pain-killers and may send you to hospital for heat treatment, manipulation or to be fitted for a collar.

Helping yourself Keeping the neck still prevents pain and allows healing. To give real benefit a collar should be worn most of the time. At night a single pillow with a deep hole punched in it will steady the head, and a small neck pillow will also help. Most cases get completely better in a few days or weeks.

BACK ACHE

This is very common from middle life onwards. Most cases are due to sprains of muscles or ligaments around the joints of the spine, to ageing changes in the discs between the vertebrae or to osteoarthritis. An active pensioner may 'slip a disc' perhaps through a burst of over-enthusiastic gardening on the first day of spring. A few cases of more severe and persistent pain are caused by conditions such as osteoporosis (page 74), Paget's Disease (pages 75–6) or secondary cancerous deposits. These are much less common and are usually easily diagnosed as they show up clearly on x-ray.

How your doctor can help Having ruled out the more serious causes, he will prescribe painkillers and rest. This produces rapid relief in most cases. If you do not get better soon he may refer you to the hospital for exercise, heat treatment, manipulation or the fitting of a corset.

Helping yourself Unless advised otherwise, the best policy is rest followed by a gradual return to normal activity. You should lie with a straight, supported spine on a firm mattress with a single pillow for most of the day until the worst of the symptoms subside. When you feel better, start to get about and resume your normal life, avoiding bending and twisting your back. If the pain recurs, slow down until it gets better and then try again.

If you are prone to back trouble you will want to take special care, doing your more energetic tasks in short periods with rest in between. It is especially important to lift with a straight back, bending your knees rather than your spine.

The glands

The body contains a number of glands which produce substances called hormones. These are carried in the blood and have widespread effects throughout the body. Hormones control the metabolism of food, growth and reproduction. If the glands secrete too much or too little of their hormones, or if the balance between them is disturbed, a general illness results. Glandular disorders usually appear gradually, with vague symptoms, and they may therefore be difficult for both doctor and patient to detect.

Common problems

THYROID DISEASE

The thyroid is a U-shaped gland at the base of the neck. Its hormone controls energy release in most body activities. Under-activity results in sluggishness, weight gain, mental dullness and apathy. Overactivity causes weight loss, heart failure and poor general health. A swelling of the thyroid gland is called a goitre. Enlargement of the whole gland is common in younger patients with overactive thyroids, but unusual in older ones. On the other hand, thyroid nodules are quite common. They nearly all consist of lumps of hardened, normal thyroid tissue and very few are cancerous.

How your doctor can help He will probably arrange for you to see a hospital specialist who will arrange tests to show the

workings of the gland, probably including a thyroid scan. For this
you will be given a substance which the thyroid can concentrate
from the blood and which has been 'tagged' with a tiny quantity
of radioactivity. Your neck will then be painlessly 'scanned' by a
machine which can build up a picture of the amount and intensity
of the radioactivity being emitted by the gland. This can show
whether lumps are active or not and also whether an enlarged
gland stretches down behind the breastbone where it may press
on vital structures.

Underactivity of the thyroid is treated by replacement of the
missing hormone, which has to be continued for life. The dose
varies from person to person and yours will be individually
tailored to your needs.

Overactivity may be treated in one or more of three ways. If
your case is non-urgent you may be admitted to hospital and
given radioactive iodine to switch off the thyroid cells. Drug
treatment works more quickly, and may be suggested if you have
heart symptoms which need rapid control. However, drugs may
cause the gland to swell, so are not used if the gland is already
enlarged or stretches down behind the breastbone. Surgery is not
often used in older people but may be necessary if a large gland is
threatening to cause pressure symptoms.

If your thyroid gland contains one or more lumps (nodules),
the scan will show whether they are 'cold' (non-functioning) or
'hot' (functioning). A biopsy may be performed to make quite
sure the lumps are benign (that is, harmless). The treatment of
benign nodules depends on whether they are causing pressure
symptoms and whether the gland as a whole is under- or over-
active.

Only one in twenty of 'cold' nodules are malignant (that is,
cancerous), and 'hot' nodules are almost never so. Thyroid
cancers are treated by surgery, radiotherapy, radioiodine or
hormones, alone or in combination.

Helping yourself People who have had treatment for an over-
active thyroid may develop under-activity of the gland in later

84

life; telling your doctor about a past illness of this sort may give him a useful clue to your present illness.

Thyroid hormone replacement must not be omitted, so it is sensible always to have a supply at hand.

DIABETES

Young diabetics grow old like the rest of us now their illness is treatable, and their ranks are swelled by those who develop the condition in later life. This is usually Type 2 diabetes, when the ageing tissues become less sensitive to insulin. If you develop Type 2 diabetes, it is unlikely to start with the dramatic symptoms of violent thirst, severe weight loss and even coma seen in Type 1 diabetes in younger people. You are more likely to be overweight than underweight, and your diabetes may be noticed because of the appearance of one of its complications. Your vision may have deteriorated or you may have developed blood vessel disease leading to angina, a heart attack or pain and ulceration in your legs. If the diabetes has affected nerve tissue, you may suffer from diarrhoea, disorders of bladder function, impotence or other sexual problems.

With the combination of poor blood supply and consequent poor healing, increased liability to infection and nerve disease giving poor feeling, some diabetics develop septic foot wounds which can go unnoticed until they become serious.

Without the help of insulin, blood sugar from the metabolism of food cannot enter the body cells. It spills over into the urine, where the extra water needed to dissolve it increases the volume of urine passed. Incontinence and dehydration can result.

This makes such alarming reading that it is important to remember that many elderly diabetics develop none of these severe problems, and no one has them all!

How your doctor can help Once he suspects you are diabetic, he can establish the fact by ordering blood and urine tests. After this he may send you to the hospital as an inpatient or outpatient for your treatment to be organized, or he may undertake this himself.

You will see a dietitian to plan a diet that is both medically suitable and easy to follow, taking account of your own eating habits and preferences. You may also be given tablets to control your blood sugar level, and in some cases insulin injections may be necessary. You will also be taught how to test your blood or urine for sugar, and told what to do if the tests show poor control.

Once your condition is stable your doctor can help you to keep as well as possible either by seeing you regularly at his own diabetic clinic or by making sure you visit the hospital clinic as often as is necessary.

Helping yourself Good control of diabetes requires careful teamwork by you and your advisers, but your efforts are the more important.

Tablets and insulin injections must be taken exactly as prescribed; the amount taken and the time of administration are both important. If you see a different doctor from usual, it is wise to tell him about your diabetes, as new tablets may interfere with your diabetic treatment. What you eat and when you eat it both matter; missing or delaying a meal may make you ill. Your diabetic control may go awry in any acute illness, especially if you are unable to eat properly.

If your blood sugar falls below normal because of illness, extra tablets or insulin or lack of food you will become hypoglycaemic. The symptoms of a 'hypo' are faintness, dizziness, mental confusion and sometimes irritability and aggression. Other people sometimes notice these more easily than the diabetic himself. If you have a 'hypo' you need sugar urgently and many diabetics carry sugar lumps or sweets at all times in case of need. If you do not raise your blood sugar, unconsciousness follows and can be dangerous. The situation can still be saved if a doctor or ambulance are called without delay, as the 'hypo' diabetic will rapidly return to normal if given glucose by injection. In case of this sort of emergency, some diabetics carry details of their diabetes and its treatment in a locket or bracelet such as those provided by the Medic-Alert Foundation (see page 169).

The best way to stop complications developing is to follow your tailor-made treatment plan religiously. In particular, make sure that your eyes are examined every six months to one year, as your doctor advises, so that diabetic retinopathy can be treated rapidly as it develops.

Meticulous foot care can prevent septic wounds from occurring. Abrupt temperature changes, as from using a hot water bottle, may damage delicate diabetic skin. Regular professional chiropody is a must. Between visits you can soften hard skin with a cream such as E45. As you wash and dry your feet daily, you can check carefully for early signs of skin breakdown and consult your doctor promptly.

The relevant patients' organization is the British Diabetic Association (see page 168).

Cancer

You may remember days when cancer was almost always thought to be a death sentence. Little could be done for it, and what treatment was available tended to be clumsy and to have so many unwanted effects that it was nearly as bad as the disease it aimed to cure.

Things are different now. Sophisticated tests mean that cancers can often be detected early, and treatment is getting more effective and less unpleasant all the time. Real cures are therefore getting commoner. What is more, we now know that older people usually get types of cancer that do not spread until late in the illness. They often do not shorten life and may cause little disability.

It is probably not helpful to think of cancer as a single disease, as there are many different types. Some are completely curable, some containable, and there are a few whose growth is difficult to stop. Even then, good care can ensure that the sufferer can continue to enjoy life right up to the time of a peaceful death.

When a cell becomes cancerous (in medical terminology

'malignant') it starts to grow and divide without regard to the needs of the rest of the body. Whereas 'benign' tumours such as warts occur because cells overgrow, the lump they form causes local symptoms only. On the other hand, the cells from a malignant primary cancer can spread to form secondary deposits, medically called metastases. These can be found some way from the primary cancer if the cells travel along blood or lymph vessels. Doctors can tell whether a tumour is formed of benign or malignant cells by examining a bit of it (a biopsy specimen) under a microscope.

If the primary and secondary cancers continue to grow, they may produce symptoms by interfering with normal body functions. Without treatment the sufferer will become more and more debilitated and vulnerable to infections and other complications, until eventually he dies. However, with modern methods of treatment this outcome can often be avoided.

How your doctor can help If his examination and tests suggest you may have cancer, he will refer you to the hospital. Here a biopsy specimen will usually be taken. How this is done will depend on where the suspected cancer is, but it is always a small procedure. The pathologist's examination will find out whether the biopsy is from a cancer, and if so, what type it is. Sometimes further tests will be organized to find out whether or not it has spread. These may include blood tests, x-rays, ultrasound or radio-isotope scans and other procedures. Whether you have to go into hospital or can have all these tests as an outpatient will depend on your individual circumstances.

At this stage your doctors will have enough information to advise you about your treatment options. Three different sorts of treatment are commonly used – surgery, radiotherapy and chemotherapy. The latter includes the use of cytotoxic drugs and hormone therapy. These may be used separately or in any combination, and which plan is best will vary from person to person. Someone you meet who seems to have the same disease as you may well have quite a different treatment plan for good technical reasons. Before you start treatment your doctors will want to make sure that your general health is as good as possible, and in particular that you are not anaemic. This will help you to withstand surgery better and give radiotherapy the best chance of killing cancerous cells.

The object of surgery is to remove the primary growth before it can cause symptoms and if possible before it has a chance to spread. The nearest lymph nodes are often removed along with the primary in case the malignant cells have already reached them. In some cases surgical treatment may give the best chance of a cure, and it often gets treatment over and done with in a single procedure. The disadvantages largely depend on what operation is necessary. Some procedures – such as the removal of a breast or formation of a stoma – may be distressing because they alter the body's shape. Most sorts of cancer surgery require a stay in hospital.

Radiotherapy and cytotoxic drugs act in the same way: they kill rapidly dividing cells. The usefulness of these treatments depends on the fact that cancer cells divide to form new cells much more rapidly than normal ones, and are therefore killed before them. Radiotherapy is now given in shorter courses spread over fewer visits than to be possible. It can also be targeted more accurately on the cancer, so unwanted effects from it damaging normal body cells are less severe than they used to be and happen less often. Treatment can be given as an outpatient if the centre is near the patient's home and he is fit enough to travel.

Cytotoxic drugs may be given in hospital, in courses with 'rests' in between. Sometimes outpatient treatment is possible (see Chapter 3).

The principle of hormone therapy is to use a hormone with *opposite* effects to the one that encourages tumour growth – for example, female hormones such as stilboestrol and related drugs are used to treat cancers of the male prostate gland. In addition steroid hormones help some complications of cancer and can improve the appetite and give a general sense of well-being.

Once you have benefited from treatment, the hospital doctors

will want to follow you up in the Outpatient Department to keep
an eye on your progress. They can then make sure you start new
treatment promptly if your cancer recurs, if you need 'running
repairs' to a stoma or develop a complication such as anaemia.
You will also be able to get treatment for any troublesome
symptoms such as pain.

Helping yourself The earlier a cancer can be diagnosed and
treated the better are the chances of curing it. It is therefore
important to see your doctor promptly if you notice anything
suspicious. Possible early signs of cancer include unexplained
lumps, ulcers that do not heal, moles that change shape or ooze,
and any unexpected bleeding – in the urine, from the back
passage, from the vagina after the menopause, or streaking of the
spit on coughing. Most of these symptoms have trivial causes
which are easily corrected, but when something more serious is
going on, the sooner it is dealt with the better.

You may want to take advantage of any available cancer
screening tests such as cervical smears or mammography (see
pages 33–4).

People with cancer vary in how much they want to know about
their condition. Your doctor may not volunteer full details, as
some patients are neither willing nor able to absorb these at once.
In general doctors are tending to explain things to their patients
more fully. You are entitled to expect an honest answer to an
honest question, and if necessary should press for the information
you want. You will probably want to understand clearly what
treatment is thought to be best for you, why this is and what
effects it is likely to have. Of course you do not have to agree to
have any investigation or treatment, but it is essential to make
sure your choice is an informed one.

If you are having radiotherapy the clinic will tell you how best
to care for your skin. The treatment area should be kept dry and
the marks that ensure the radiotherapy is directed accurately at
the cancer should not be disturbed. Adhesive plasters or powders
containing zinc oxide attract radiation, so should not be used on

the treatment area. The treated skin will become a little fragile, so it is best not to scratch it if possible.

The unwanted effects of radiotherapy and of cytotoxic drugs are similar, but they do not always happen. The commonest symptoms are tiredness, lethargy and loss of appetite, sometimes with sickness. In a way these are good signs, because they are thought to show that the cancer cells are dead or dying, but they are unpleasant to experience. Drinking extra fluid can help, and your appetite may be tempted by small, frequent meals, preceded by a little of your favourite alcoholic drink. If you tell your doctors how you feel, they may be able to prescribe something to help or to organize a short break in your treatment until your body has settled down.

If you have radiotherapy to your head or receive some sorts of cytotoxic drugs your hair may fall out. It may help to wear a net or turban at night to catch lost hair, and to use a satin pillowslip to reduce rubbing. The hair almost always regrows once the treatment stops. If this does not happen or if growth is slow a wig can be supplied by the NHS, or you may prefer to buy your own.

As with other illnesses, most people with cancer feel better if they can do something to help themselves, rather than passively allowing things to be done to them. The British Association of Cancer United Patients (BACUP) can provide clearly written information leaflets for you to read and absorb at leisure. These describe the commoner sorts of cancer and give general information on living with the disease and its treatment, including sensible advice on diet. Some cancer patients like to meet people who are coping with similar problems of their own, and BACUP can give details of such support groups. There are also self-help organizations for sufferers from cancer in particular sites, such as the Breast Care and Mastectomy Association for breast cancer sufferers (see page 167).

Various 'alternative therapies' for cancer are available. If you are a cancer patient, it is obviously sensible to keep your general health as good as possible, and spiritual well-being is an important part of this. Time and trouble spent on whatever helps you in this respect is probably well spent. However, it is wise to be wary of unorthodox treatments that seem to offer a cure, for a number of reasons. In the first place, none of these have been shown to work, and they may delay or interfere with effective treatment. Second, some regimes – those involving special diets, for instance – can be actively harmful to health, causing excess weight loss and containing unwisely large doses of vitamins. Third, 'alternative therapies' may be expensive in money and also in time, which may be the most precious thing to a cancer patient and his family.

You will probably have extra expenses because of your illness, and may be entitled to state benefits such as a financial contribution towards travelling costs. Services such as Home Help or Meals on Wheels may be useful to you if you are feeling unwell. The medical social worker at the hospital, or your local DSS office or Citizens' Advice Bureau will help you find out what you can claim.

You may find the practical aspects of coping with cancer easier than coming to terms with your feelings about it. Many people are numbed with shock when told they have cancer, and may be unable to take it in, denying the true nature of their illness. Anger is a common feeling and is often directed against doctors, nurses or family members. You may want to blame someone for your illness, or feel guilty about it yourself and perhaps withdraw to 'lick your wounds' in solitude.

Coming to terms with your illness will be easier if you can talk to someone about it, and the people who are fond of you will also need sympathetic listeners. It helps to talk openly with someone who will not be shocked and upset by what you say – a friend, doctor, nurse or other carer or a minister of religion – whoever suits you best. If there is no one suitable in your circle, BACUP may be able to help.

It is usually best to tell those close to you the facts of your illness. Both relatives and cancer patients themselves may try to keep the news from each other. This usually seems to be a mistake and leads to unnecessary misunderstanding and loneliness. Children in particular need as much of the truth as they are able to understand. They are bound to notice something is wrong, and if not told the facts, are likely to imagine far worse explanations than the real one.

Common types of cancer

LUNG

Strictly speaking, the tumour is usually in the bronchus, one of the airways. Common signs are a persistent cough which may produce bloodstained spit, chest pain and wheezing. Later the sufferer loses weight and may show signs of tumour spread.

A chest x-ray and examination of cells from a spit sample may confirm the diagnosis. Bronchoscopy may be necessary, a special telescope being passed down the windpipe under general or local anaesthetic so that the suspect tissue can be inspected and sampled. When the possible tumour is near the chest wall, a biopsy can sometimes be obtained through the skin using a needle or drill. Further tests may be performed to look for secondary spread.

Surgical removal of the tumour is not often possible in older people. Radiotherapy often relieves symptoms by shrinking tumours causing pressure, pain or bleeding. Cytotoxic drugs are rarely used.

BREAST

This is the commonest tumour of retired women. Sufferers usually notice a lump in the breast. Other signs, occurring with or without a lump, are change in breast size or shape, dimpling of its skin, enlargement of its veins or the appearance of a swelling in the armpit. Changes in the nipple are significant, such as the appearance of a crusting rash, a bloodstained discharge or its turning inwards to form a dent rather than a peak.

Once a breast lump has been found, fluid or a small portion of tissue is taken from it for examination and special x-rays called mammograms are performed. Nine out of ten breast lumps are found to be harmless. If cancer is found, tests for spread are likely to include a bone scan and an ultrasound scan of the liver.

Treatment involves different combinations of surgery, radiotherapy and drugs depending on individual circumstances. Operations in general are smaller and less mutilating than they used to be. BACUP's Cancer Information Service produce a booklet called *Understanding Cancer of the Breast*, and the Breast Care and Mastectomy Association provides information for women who have had breast surgery.

BOWEL

Early signs are bleeding from the back passage and a change in the normal bowel habit. Later the sufferer may feel generally unwell, lose appetite and weight and develop abdominal pain or discomfort.

Likely diagnostic tests include a barium enema, in which a thick white liquid is injected up the back passage to outline the bowel lining on x-ray. Also a modified telescope (sigmoidoscope or colonoscope) can be used to inspect the diseased area and take a sample of the suspicious tissue for laboratory examination.

A bowel cancer is usually removed surgically. If possible the cut ends of the gut are joined up so that stools can still pass in the usual way. When this cannot be done a colostomy is formed (see Stomas, pages 50–52).

WOMB AND CERVIX

Cancer can occur in the womb proper (body of the uterus) or in the cervix where it opens into the vagina. The commonest symptom is abnormal vaginal bleeding, either starting again in a woman past the menopause or occurring between periods in a younger woman.

Cervical cancer or pre-cancer may be diagnosed from a cervical smear, when the most superficial layer of cells are painlessly scraped off for laboratory examination. Further biopsy and sometimes examination under anaesthesia is then necessary to find the extent of the disease. Cancer of the body of the uterus can only be diagnosed by examining scrapings of its lining, so examination under anaesthesia is again necessary.

Treatment may be by cautery, laser, surgery, radiotherapy or a combination of these, aiming to destroy or remove the abnormal cells. A radium implant may provide the radiation. This is inserted under anaesthetic and left in place to do its work for a measured number of hours before removal. During this time the patient needs to stay in her hospital bed and visiting may be restricted to prevent accidental radiation to family and friends. As soon as the implant is removed the patient can again mix normally.

PROSTATE

Cancer of the prostate produces the same symptoms as benign enlargement of the gland – difficulty with and increased frequency of passing urine, a poor stream and sometimes blood-staining of urine. Four out of five patients with these symptoms have benign enlargement only, but it is sensible to consult your doctor promptly as further examination and tests may be necessary to tell for certain. He will refer you to the hospital, where the surgeon will feel your prostate using his gloved finger inserted up your back passage. He will probably take a needle biopsy under a local anaesthetic and organize further blood tests, x-rays and scans.

If you are found to have prostatic cancer, your treatment will be tailored to your particular circumstances. The tumour grows slowly and may need no treatment at first, though careful regular follow-up examinations will be organized in case action is needed later. If surgery is decided on, the usual operation is the trans-urethral resection (TUR), using a slender instrument passed up through the penis under general or spinal anaesthesia. Radio-therapy may be used for the original tumour and is also especially helpful in relieving bone pain from secondary spread. Hormone therapy is often effective as prostatic cancer depends on male hormones for its growth. Tablets which reduce the amount of male hormone may be given, or alternatively female hormones which oppose its action are used. Hormone treatment may cause impotence (inability to have an erection), shrinking of the genitals and enlargement and tenderness of the male breasts. All these unwanted effects tend to get better if and when hormone treatment stops. In the meantime you may well feel upset; try discussing the situation with your doctor or the surgeon in the first instance. You will be able to get accurate and confidential information on continuing your sex life from SPOD (see page 170).

Very occasionally, either the prostatic cancer or its treatment can cause incontinence. If you are unlucky enough to develop this, it may help to read the relevant section of this book and to seek help from your doctor, the practice nurse or continence adviser (see pages 149–50).

BLADDER

Blood in the urine is the commonest sign of cancer of the bladder, sometimes together with pain in the lower part of the abdomen or the private parts. Repeated urinary infections also occur.

After you consult your family doctor he will refer you to hospital for further tests. These will include a cystoscopy, in which a very slender telescope is passed up your urethra, to inspect the bladder lining. A general or local anaesthetic is given for this. Through the cystoscope the inside of your bladder can be inspected and samples can be taken of any tissue that looks abnormal. An IVP (special kidney x-ray) is also likely to be performed.

Treatment involves the surgical removal of the tumour or tumours. This can nearly always be done through the cystoscope without the need for an open operation. Cytotoxic drugs are occasionally put in the bladder to help prevent regrowth, and radiotherapy is sometimes added.

Having once had a bladder cancer, you will need to attend the hospital for further follow-up cystoscopies for the rest of your life. This is done because of the risk of recurrence, which can be nipped in the bud if diagnosed and treated early.

It is worth remembering that many bladder tumours are comparatively harmless and that this system of treatment is very effective. Many bladder cancer sufferers lead long, full and healthy lives and eventually die of something quite unrelated to their cancer.

SKIN

Cancer on the skin forms lumps, warty masses or ulcers which grow slowly and do not heal. It is sensible to show your doctor any such skin abnormality which does not get better within three weeks.

The commonest skin cancer is the rodent ulcer, almost always found on the face. Much rarer and more serious is the malignant melanoma, usually forming as a cancerous change in a mole already present in the patient. The mole grows, darkens and may ulcerate or bleed. Pigment may stream out from it into the surrounding skin like a comet's tail.

Skin cancers are usually treated surgically, though radiotherapy is also used. With a melanoma a wide margin of tissue is usually taken from around the growth to be sure all the cancer is removed. A much smaller operation is usually necessary for other sorts of skin cancer, and a complete cure is usual.

Nearly all skin lumps and ulcers prove to be benign. When skin cancer is present, however, it is worth catching early so that the surgical scar is as small and inconspicuous as possible.

*

'What do you expect at your age?' Should this be said to you when you are unwell, you would be right to reply that you expect the cause to be found and as far as possible removed. Like those of any other age, old people become unwell when something has gone wrong with them; in other words, 'You're ill because you're ill, not because you're old.'

3

Your Medicines:
What They Are and How to Use Them

This chapter is divided into two parts. If you are taking any medicines, you are likely to find the first part, 'General knowledge about medicines', interesting and useful. It includes information about generic and trade names of drugs, and the difference between the sort of medicines that can only be obtained with a doctor's prescription and the type that can be bought 'over the counter'. This is followed by an account of the different preparations in which medicines are made up and how they should be used. Next come suggestions on getting the most from your medicines, both by your own efforts and with help from doctors, pharmacists and nurses. The first part ends with hints on storage of medicines, coping with drug treatment while away from home, and avoiding the pitfalls of repeat prescriptions.

Specific types of commonly used medicines are discussed in the second part, with details of their common uses and possible unwanted effects. To use this information you will need to know the type of medicine you are taking – whether it is a diuretic, an anti-inflammatory agent or an antibiotic, for instance. The doctor or pharmacist will be able to tell you this.

General knowledge about medicines

What is a drug?
'Taking drugs' to many people means doing something illegal and possibly dangerous. To a doctor or pharmacist, however, a 'drug' is any chemical used for treatment. Taking an aspirin for a

headache or even sucking a peppermint to relieve indigestion could technically be described as 'taking drugs'. To avoid this sort of misunderstanding, many doctors and pharmacists now try to talk about 'medicines' rather than 'drugs' when discussing prescribed treatment. In practice though you may still find the words 'drug' and 'medicine' used interchangeably.

Generic and trade names
Every medicine has a generic name, which is usually a shortened form of its chemical name. Each company that manufactures the medicine will then attach its own trade or brand name. In general, doctors are encouraged to prescribe by generic names. This is because generic drugs are usually cheaper than the branded version. Sometimes, however, the doctor will specify a medicine by its brand name because he knows that particular preparation is better absorbed, quicker-acting or of more consistently reliable quality than others. This is rather like buying whatever sort of lavatory paper is cheapest at the supermarket this week (generic lavatory paper), while buying a particular brand of baked beans you prefer, rather than the supermarket's cheaper generic version.

It is worth remembering that different brands of the same generic medicine may look quite different – for instance, tablets may be of different shape or colour. Check with the doctor or pharmacist if your usual medicine appears different, as this may be the explanation.

'Unwanted' effects
If you are over sixty, almost all the medicines now in common use have been developed in your lifetime. Modern medicines are powerful, both in curing illnesses that used to be fatal and in relieving unpleasant symptoms, but they can also themselves cause symptoms. It is probably better to talk about unwanted effects rather than side effects, as many medicines have more than one effect; which is wanted and which unwanted may vary from one occasion to another.

Effective drugs are like sharp knives: if used carelessly, or with the intent of hurting someone, or if the user has poor sight or dexterity, great harm can result. In any case, the damage caused is not the fault of the medicine or the knife, but of the person using it or who made it available. There is no such thing as a good drug or a bad drug, only one that is used well or badly.

Older people are especially prone to the unwanted effects of medicines. One reason for this is that medicines are metabolized and removed from the body more slowly as age advances. A normal adult dose of a medicine may accumulate to toxic levels in an older person if it is taken daily. In general older people need lower doses of medicine than people half their age. Mistakes in taking correctly prescribed medicines can also happen, and the risk of this is greater when the person in charge of the medicines is forgetful, cannot see well or has difficulty in opening the package.

If you think a medicine you are taking may be affecting you badly, it is as well to see your doctor as soon as possible. Some medicines should not be stopped suddenly; steroids, drugs for Parkinson's Disease, medicines to prevent epilepsy and some others come into this category. If you have to wait a day or two to see your doctor, it is wise to ask him or her over the telephone whether or not you should go on taking the medicine in the meantime.

Finding a balance

Whenever medicines are prescribed and taken, the likely benefits have to be balanced against the possible ill-effects of treatment. In some severe illnesses the risk of not using a medicine is greater than that of doing so even when unwanted effects may also be grave, and it is the doctor's job to know enough about both illnesses and medicines to explain the situation to the patient and his relatives on these occasions. In many cases of milder illness the decision is less clear-cut. The patient's point of view on other drawbacks of treatment becomes very relevant here; these include the inconvenience of obtaining the medicine and of reorganizing daily life so that it can be taken reliably, as well as the change of role into that of 'sick person'. Only you can know how badly you want treatment; on the one hand your symptoms may need immediate relief, while on the other a simple explanation of what is going on may be enough. On the whole the decision-making process is quicker, easier and more friendly if both parties communicate clearly with each other. It is of course up to you whether you take the offered advice, but it is sensible to be sure you understand the reasons for the doctor's suggested treatment before deciding against it.

Types of medicine

Prescription-only medicines (sometimes labelled PoM)
These are available only on a doctor's prescription. Some are called 'controlled drugs' and are subject to the regulations of the Misuse of Drugs Act. Morphine is an example of a controlled drug.

Over-the-counter medicines
These come in two types:

- Those which can only be sold in a pharmacy with a qualified pharmacist in the shop.
- Those which are available in other shops such as super-markets, as well as at the chemist's. Simple household remedies such as mild painkillers and indigestion mixtures come in this category.

It is best not to rely on self-medication for more than a few days. Most minor ailments get better within this time, and those that do not need a doctor's opinion. If you are already taking prescribed medicines, you may wish to discuss your choice of over-the-counter medicines with the pharmacist to make sure all your medicines are compatible.

Drug preparations
Active medicines come in many different forms. Sometimes the substance has to be given in a particular way, but if you have

practical difficulty in using one preparation, it is worth asking your doctor if it or a good substitute comes in a more convenient form.

Tablets or capsules
These are perhaps the commonest preparation. They are usually designed to be swallowed whole with a good draught of water; in some cases milk will interfere with the tablet's action. If you find it difficult to swallow your tablets whole, it may be acceptable to chew them up with a mouthful of food. Check with your doctor or pharmacist first, however, as some tablets cannot be treated in this way.

Liquids
These are easier to swallow than tablets but more difficult to carry about. You may find antacid tablets a useful alternative to the liquid for pocket or handbag.

Sublingual preparations
Some tablets though put in the mouth are not swallowed but allowed to dissolve under the tongue; glyceryl trinitrate is often taken in this way to relieve angina. The medicine is then absorbed directly into the bloodstream to do its work, whereas only an unpredictable amount is delivered if the drug is swallowed. Glyceryl trinitrate is sometimes sprayed into the mouth to be absorbed in the same way.

Inhaled medicines
Various sorts are used for chest diseases; the idea is to get the medicine to its site of action with the minimum of waste and unwanted effects in the rest of the body. The medicine may fail to work if the inhaler is not used properly, and some are only easy when you know how: something as simple as failing to synchronize breathing and spraying can sabotage treatment. If you are prescribed an inhaler, it is sensible to get someone (doctor, nurse or pharmacist) to show you how to use it and then to check that you are doing so correctly.

Locally applied medicines

There is a knack to administering eye drops and eye ointments. The practice or district nurse should be asked for advice and guidance in doing this. Other topical (locally applied) medicines include ointments or creams and the newer plaster patches impregnated with glyceryl trinitrate or with hormones. Topical medicines can be as powerful for good or ill as those that are swallowed. It is important to make sure you know exactly how to use them, for example where on the body patches should be applied, when they should be attached and removed and whether or not ointments and creams on the skin should be covered with dressings.

Injections

These are usually given by doctors or nurses rather than by patients themselves. An exception is insulin, often self-administered by diabetics. Insulin-requiring diabetics are always taught how to give their own injections and usually become very skilled at it. They may need to ask for help if they become less able to manage because of worsening sight or dexterity.

Rectal or vaginal medicines

In continental countries such as France the rectal route is more often used than in the UK to supply a medicine that needs slow absorption into the body. In Britain these routes are more often used to treat local conditions such as colitis or constipation. Suppositories (for the rectum) and pessaries (for the vagina) are solid preparations which are usually bulkier than tablets designed to be swallowed. They are meant to dissolve slowly after insertion releasing the contained medicine gradually. Rectal and vaginal medicines also come as creams or foams, in a variety of applications. If you are prescribed a rectal or vaginal medicine, you may need to ask the doctor, nurse or pharmacist exactly how to apply it.

Getting the most from your medicines

Help from other people

Your doctor

Drug treatment will work best if you and your doctor manage it together as a partnership. For this to be successful, good communications are essential. You need to *tell* your doctor:

- *what medicines you are taking already*, whether prescribed or over the counter. The practice should keep a record of your current treatment, but it does no harm to keep your own list. It is important to mention any medicines not ordered by your own doctor but prescribed elsewhere or bought by you over the counter. Do be honest if, for instance, you have stopped taking something your doctor has prescribed or if you have consulted an alternative practitioner; failure to do this might lead to unwanted effects from medicines that do not mix.
- *whether you are allergic to any medicine* (for example, penicillin) or have suffered ill-effects from medicines in the past. The doctor can then avoid this happening again if similar treatment is necessary.

You may like to *ask* your doctor the following questions about any medicine he or she prescribes:

- *'What is its name?'* A generic name as well as a trade name will be useful.
- *'What sort of medicine is it?'* for example, a painkiller, an anti-inflammatory agent, or an antibiotic.
- *'What do you expect it to do for me?'* This will tell you what to expect – for instance, that your pain will be relieved, or that excess water will leave your body as a larger than usual amount of urine.
- *'What unwanted effects should I look out for?'* Sleepiness, rashes and digestive disturbances are the commonest, but there may be others, depending on what medicine is taken.
- *'What should I do if these occur?'* You will need to know

whether to report to the doctor at once, and whether or not to
continue with the medicine in the meantime.

- *'How should I take the medicine?'* This includes:
- o *'By what route?'* Regrettably, the occasional rectal suppository
  is swallowed!
- o *'How many times a day?'* If you are taking medicines already,
  ask your doctor to arrange the simplest possible regime to
  include them all.
- o *'Before or after food?'* Some medicines are rendered ineffective
  by food, while others may be harmful on an empty stomach.
- o *'Do I take it every day, or just to relieve a bothersome
  symptom?'* Some medicines prevent illness, while others are
  taken only when necessary.
- o *'How much do I take at a time?'* You may particularly want to
  know whether you can safely increase the dose or frequency,
  or whether it would be dangerous to do so. It is worth
  remembering that older bodies often need smaller drug doses
  than younger ones.
- o *'For how long do I take it?'* You will want to know whether (a)
  you need to finish the bottle; for an antibiotic to get rid of an
  infection, the full course has to be taken; (b) you need only to
  take the medicine until you feel better; (c) you should persevere
  with treatment until you next see the doctor, and when this
  should be; (d) you need a further supply when you have
  finished your current one.
- o *'What should I do if I miss a dose?'* In general the best course is
  to take the next dose at the usual time, and not to take a double
  dose.
- o *'Do I need to change my living habits?'* Some medicines do not
  mix with alcohol or with certain foods; others may cause
  drowsiness which may affect your driving. Your doctor should
  warn you about this, and the pharmacist is likely to put an
  extra label on your bottle of medicine.

Your pharmacist
It is usually wise to find a friendly and helpful pharmacist within a

convenient distance, and then to take all your custom to that shop.

Your pharmacist should:

- add to your doctor's information as to when and how to take your medicine.
- tell you how to store it. Some medicines need to be kept in a refrigerator and others to be protected from light in a dark glass bottle. This may be important if you had planned to put some of your tablets in another container such as a 'memory box'.
- tell you how long it will keep. Some eye ointments and eyedrops have a short lifespan after opening.
- tell you how to dispose of unwanted medicines. Small quantities of liquids and tablets can be flushed down the lavatory. The pharmacist can tell you what to do with other sorts (for example, aerosols) or may offer to get rid of them for you.
- advise you about over-the-counter medicines, for example, which ones are likely to suit you and can be mixed safely with your prescribed medicines.

Your medicines should come in packaging that you can open easily; tell the pharmacist if you have difficulty with child-resistant tops or blister packs. Bottles with prominent flanges on their caps may be available, and are very useful to arthritis sufferers.

If you are taking a liquid medicine, the pharmacist should provide you with a standard spoon or marked plastic cup to measure the dose.

The nurse

Some hospitals sensibly make sure their patients can cope with medication after they go home by teaching them to look after their medicines while still in the ward and under nursing supervision.

If you have problems coping with your medicines at home, the practice nurse or health visitor may be able to help, for example, by labelling them with larger letters or in working out a system for jogging your memory.

Helping yourself

Speak up
Do ask for information or help whenever you need it; this is useful to you, and also prompts doctors and others to give information unasked to people who may not be as well informed or assertive as you are.

'Compliance'
Many of us, young and old, find it difficult to remember to take our medicines exactly as directed – what doctors and pharmacists call 'compliance'. Ways of helping your compliance might include:

- Ensuring your medicines are *labelled so that you can read and understand the information*: the type of chemists' labels may be too small and faint to read easily. A nurse or pharmacist can help you to compose something like 'heart pill – one each morning' and write it on a luggage label in thick felt pen. (Braille labels can be obtained from the RNIB if needed.) Make sure your labelling, once attached, does not obscure the pharmacists' technical information (proper name of drug and amount in the dose), as this is very useful to any doctor who treats you in an emergency.
- Making a *master chart* of your daily medication, with specimens of your tablets attached by sticky tape alongside a note of the times at which they should be taken.
- Ruling up a *hospital-type drug chart*, in which every dose of a medicine is ticked off as it is taken. This is most useful for someone leading a busy life with irregular commitments who has to take a short course of a medicine like an antibiotic.
- Using a *memory device* to help you remember to take your medicines. At the simplest level, you can put your day's ration

of pills into a box or egg cup first thing in the morning, while you remember. A step up from this is to use a different coloured container for each time of day – morning, lunchtime or evening. Specially designed 'memory boxes' of various degrees of complexity are available; one type has seven boxes, each subdivided into four and contained in a wallet, to hold a week's tablets. But think carefully before you buy one of these: not all are easy to use if you suffer from arthritis or another complaint which interferes with finger movement. Also, some medicines do not keep well outside their original containers.

Repeat prescriptions

It is sometimes very convenient to ask the doctor to send you a repeat prescription for a medicine by post. Do not be tempted to do this too many times, however; it is wise for anyone taking medicines regularly to have a medical check *at least* every six months. The medicine can then be stopped if, as often happens, it is no longer necessary. Many practices now operate a recall system to avoid repeat prescriptions that 'run and run'.

Safe storage

This is important enough for the well-known rules to be repeated.

It is easy to forget how agile and inquisitive small children are when they are infrequent visitors rather than permanent residents. It is always sensible to check round the house for medicines as well as other hazards when small relatives or friends are expected.

Do not throw unwanted medicines into the dustbin, where they may get into the wrong hands. Instead empty bottles down the lavatory or take the contents to the pharmacist for disposal.

Resist the temptation to share medicines with a friend whose symptoms seem to be the same as yours. In fact, both your illnesses and the way your bodies react to the medicine may be widely different.

Do not keep medicines indefinitely. Some become useless after a time, while others can actually be dangerous.

Away from home

Before your holiday, make sure that you have enough of your medicines to last until you return home. As an added precaution, note down the details of your medication and your doctor's telephone number in case you need replacements in unforeseen circumstances. If you are in the UK, you could ask a local GP to write you a prescription for further supplies. Alternatively, a pharmacist may sell you up to five days' supply, but only if he or she is convinced you know what medicines you should be taking; this may be expensive.

If you are going abroad by air, it is wise to keep your medicines with you in your hand luggage. Replacements will be more difficult to obtain than in Britain, as in other countries your medicines may be known by different names. It is far better to make sure the situation does not arise by making careful preparations before leaving home.

Some commonly used medicines

These are discussed under the appropriate body system. Exceptions are antibiotics, steroid treatment, vitamins and treatment for cancer, each of which is covered in a separate section towards the end of the chapter.

For treating heart and blood vessel diseases

Cardiac glycosides (for example, digoxin)

These slow the heart rate by damping down some disordered rhythms. They also increase the efficiency of a heart which is under strain.

Unwanted effects include loss of appetite, sickness and vomiting and heart rhythm disturbance. These are more likely in people with a low blood potassium level. (See Diuretics.)

Digoxin and similar drugs are taken regularly, rather than when particular symptoms occur.

Diuretics (for example, bendrofluazide, frusemide, amiloride, triamterene)

These make the kidneys remove extra salt and water from the blood, so that blood volume and pressure fall and excess water is withdrawn from the tissues to restore them. Diuretics are used to lower high blood pressure or to get rid of watery swelling (medical term 'oedema') from the body, especially when it is interfering with lung function. Reducing blood volume lowers the amount of work the heart has to do, so diuretics may be helpful in heart failure.

Some types of diuretic lower blood potassium (chemical symbol K), and it may be necessary to take replacement potassium to prevent muscle weakness, confusion and unsteadiness from the chemical disturbance. Some diuretic preparations (often with a K in the name) include potassium in the tablet.

Diabetes and gout may be made worse by some diuretics. Urine flow of course increases as the excess water is got rid of; this may cause urinary retention in older men with enlarged prostate glands, or lead to incontinence in anyone whose urinary control is less than perfect. Diuretic users are occasionally troubled by stomach upsets, skin rashes or impotence.

Diuretics are taken regularly, usually early in the day so that the extra need to pass water does not interfere with the night's rest. Diuretic treatment started during an acute illness such as an episode of heart failure can often be stopped once it has passed.

Beta-blockers (for example, propranolol, oxprenol, atenolol, metoprolol, timolol)

These affect the function of the heart and blood vessels by blocking the action of adrenalin at some nerve endings. Adrenalin is produced in the body in small quantities in normal circumstances and in larger amounts under stress conditions. It is responsible for many of the body changes we associate with anger and fear, such as a pounding heart, dry mouth and dilated pupils. By opposing these changes, beta-blockers can be used in the treatment of high blood pressure, to prevent angina by reducing the heart's work and thus its need for oxygen, and to protect the heart from the effects of an overactive thyroid gland. Someone who has had a heart attack may be given a beta-blocker to prevent a recurrence or to control heart rhythm disturbances. Symptoms of anxiety like palpitations and tremor can also be controlled by beta-blockers.

Unwanted effects include undue slowing of the heart, cardiac failure, wheezing, chest tightness, cold hands and feet, stomach upsets, sleep disturbances and nightmares. They may lower blood pressure enough to cause fatigue and exhaustion, and may mask the symptoms of hypoglycaemia in diabetics.

Vasodilators (for example, nitrates such as glyceryl trinitrate and isosorbide dinitrate; calcium channel blockers such as nifedipine and diltiazem)
These expand blood vessels (that is, cause vasodilation).

Glyceryl trinitrate (GTN) has a rapid action in relieving angina, but its effect is short-lived (twenty to thirty minutes). It is useful if taken before exertion or by people who have infrequent symptoms. It cannot be swallowed in the usual way, as an unpredictable amount is made inactive by the liver. However, it reaches the circulation rapidly if absorbed from the mouth, either when a tablet is placed under the tongue and allowed to dissolve or when an aerosol spray is used to deliver a measured amount of GTN. Tablets and aerosols are used as necessary in this way to relieve symptoms.

GTN is also available in impregnated plasters or as ointments. These are useful to *prevent* symptoms in people who are woken by chest pain during the night. They must be used exactly as directed.

People with frequent angina symptoms may do better on regular treatment aiming to prevent attacks. Alternatives are also needed for people who find nitrates difficult to take or their unwanted effects intolerable. Some patients take beta-blockers, which reduce the heart's need for oxygen. Others are better suited by 'calcium channel-blockers' which interfere with the chemical changes that accompany heart action; this depresses the heart's activity. As calcium channel-blockers also dilate the blood vessels and lower the blood pressure, they can be used to treat hypertension as well.

Nitrates may cause an uncomfortable feeling of fullness in the head, or fainting because of the fall in blood pressure. These can sometimes be avoided by using GTN tablets or spray in a sitting position and by spitting out tablet remains as soon as the angina pain is relieved.

The unwanted effects of calcium channel-blockers vary from one preparation to another. In general they happen because the heart's action is depressed too much, causing heart failure and rhythm disturbances. Other symptoms are due to vasodilatation and include faintness, flushing, headache and swollen ankles.

Vasodilators have occasionally been tried as a treatment to improve the blood supply to the legs in patients with arterial disease. Unfortunately they do not usually seem to help much, neither do they benefit brain function in patients with multi-infarct dementia (mental impairment due to chronically poor brain blood supply).

Anticoagulants (for example, heparin, warfarin)
These are used to prevent a blood clot from forming or if already there, from spreading further. This is especially likely to happen on the slower-moving, venous side of the circulation, notably in the deep veins of the legs. People prone to clotting disorders who may require anticoagulants include some patients undergoing surgery and those with artificial heart valves.

When immediate effects are required, heparin is given by injection, as warfarin by mouth takes thirty-six to forty-eight hours to have a full effect against blood clotting. The patient's blood is regularly tested to see how fast it clots, and the dose of anticoagulant altered in the light of test results. Other medicines may alter the effect of anticoagulants, so any prescribing doctor needs to know what the patient is already taking. Patients should carry an anticoagulant card with details of their therapy and how it is controlled; this should be shown to any new doctor.

The main unwanted effects are bleeding from the gut, bladder or other sources.

Aspirin, dipyridamole and other 'antiplatelet drugs' interfere with blood clotting in a different way. They are sometimes used in patients who have suffered transient ischaemic attacks (TIAs) to prevent a full-blown stroke, or to prevent a second heart attack. A new development to reduce the damage a heart attack does is to inject a substance to dissolve the clots in the coronary arteries and enable the blood to reach the heart muscle again. These injections have to be given within two hours of the start of the heart attack.

For diseases of the lungs and airways

Bronchodilators (for example, salbutamol, terbutaline)
These expand the airways (bronchi) and thus allow more air into the lungs. They are often delivered into the air passages through inhalers. If an inhaler is not used properly the patient will not get the full benefit of the medicine, so it is very important to learn how to use an inhaler correctly. In a common type the user breathes in slowly at the same time as he releases the medicine into the mouth as an aerosol; he then holds his breath for ten seconds to allow the bronchodilator to act. Some inhalers are activated by an inward breath, and these may be easier to use.

Unwanted effects include trembling, nervousness, headache and a fast heart beat.

Bronchodilators can also be taken orally. Sustained release theophylline and aminophylline are sometimes useful to control wheezing at night and in the early morning.

Unwanted effects include palpitations, gastrointestinal upsets and disturbed sleep.

Rectal suppositories are another slow-release form of bronchodilator.

Unwanted effects may cause inflammation of the back passage.

Cough mixtures

To *suppress a cough* (for example, codeine, pholcodine) People cough to clear their lungs of spit and phlegm. If this normal reflex is suppressed, phlegm may accumulate and clog the lungs. Cough suppressants are therefore only used to prevent a *dry* cough which is interfering with sleep or is distressing a very ill patient.

The most tiresome unwanted effect for most people is constipation. In a frail person the drive to go on breathing may be dangerously reduced.

To promote coughing and clear the chest (for example, expectorant mixtures) A variety of these are available. They are cheap and harmless, but there is little evidence that any of them work. Simple steam inhalations are more useful. It is not necessary to add anything to the water, though a scenting agent such as Friar's Balsam can be used if liked.

For diseases of the digestive system

Antacids (for example, aluminium hydroxide preparations, magnesium carbonate or trisilicate)
These are often useful for dyspepsia, whether or not a peptic ulcer is present. Antacids are taken as necessary when symptoms occur or are expected, up to four times or more a day. Liquid preparations are more effective than tablets but less easy to carry around. In general, magnesium compounds have a mild laxative effect, while aluminium ones tend to constipate.

Unwanted effects are rarely important in healthy people. Those on low-salt diets or anyone suffering from kidney disease or heart failure should ask the doctor or pharmacist which antacid preparation is safe for them to take. Antacids may also interfere with the absorption of other medicines.

Antispasmodics (for example, propantheline, peppermint oils)
These are occasionally used to relieve symptoms in diverticular disease and other bowel conditions.

Propantheline and similar medicines may cause difficulty in passing urine, especially in men with prostatic symptoms, acute glaucoma in susceptible people, dry mouth, flushing and confusion. They need to be used with great care in older people. Peppermint oil has none of these unwanted effects, though it may occasionally cause heartburn.

Ulcer-healing medicines

Reducing acid-secretion (for example, ranitidine, cimetidine) These block the nerves that cause acid to be secreted, and thus allow the ulcer to heal. H_2 receptor-blocking drugs, as they are called technically, are usually given in short courses, though a maintenance dose is sometimes used.

Unwanted effects are rare with ranitidine; occasionally an older patient becomes confused, recovering when the medicine is stopped. Ill-effects are not common with cimetidine either, but diarrhoea, dizziness, rashes, confusion and impotence can occur.

Protecting the stomach and duodenal lining (for example, bismuth chelate, sucralfate, carbenoxolone) Bismuth chelate is taken regularly as a twenty-eight-day course. It may act by coating the ulcer or perhaps by stimulating bicarbonate secretion. The patient taking bismuth should not eat for two hours before and half an hour after a dose, as if he does the medicine will stick to the food rather than to the ulcer.

Unwanted effects are only severe in patients with poor kidney function. In others, bismuth can cause a tendency to constipation and it also darkens stools; this looks alarming but is harmless. Sucralfate is given in courses as necessary; it can also cause constipation.

Carbenoxolone is a derivative of liquorice and protects the stomach lining against attack by acid.

Salt and water retention may cause heart failure and a rise in blood pressure. Because of this, carbenoxolone is rarely used in older people.

For hiatus hernia
When this causes reflux oesophagitis, antacids may be prescribed, often combined with an alginate; this bland compound floats on

the stomach contents and is thus more likely than stomach acid to flow back into the gullet. It may also coat and protect the sore area. In another compound the antacid is combined with a local anaesthetic to reduce pain.

These preparations are taken as required and very rarely cause unwanted effects. Should they prove ineffective, medicines reducing acid-secretion may be tried.

Medicines for stoma patients

If you have a stoma it is important that you mention it to any doctor who may treat you without knowing about it, as special care is needed in prescribing medicines. 'Enteric coated' and 'slow-release' preparations are not usually suitable; they are designed to liberate their contained drug slowly as they pass down the gut, and are not able to do so adequately in the shortened intestine of a stoma patient. The effects of antacids in increasing or decreasing bowel action are also exaggerated.

Patients with an ileostomy are especially vulnerable to dehydration if they are given enemas, bowel washouts or strong laxatives (before some x-ray procedures, for example). This can also happen if they take diuretics, when potassium levels also fall; this can be dangerous in people taking digoxin.

Constipation may trouble a colostomy patient who is taking strong painkillers. It should get better if fluid intake and the amount of fibre in the diet are increased. If necessary, bulk-forming laxatives or the smallest possible dose of a senna preparation may be added.

On the other hand, iron preparations may cause loose stools and skin irritation, and iron may need to be given intramuscularly. In general, diarrhoea can be helped by substances that slow down gut muscle action, such as codeine phosphate, loperamide and diphenoxylate. Bulk-forming agents sometimes help, but it can be difficult to get the dose quite right.

Advice on stoma care products is best obtained from the stoma care nurse (see page 150).

For gallstones

A minority of patients have the sort of gallstones that can be dissolved by giving bile acids by mouth (for example, cheno-deoxycholic or ursodeoxycholic acid).

Unwanted effects include diarrhoea, skin rashes and minor disturbances of the liver. The stones may reform after treatment with bile acids is stopped.

For constipation

Laxatives

Many older people have a long-standing tendency to constipation, and they often buy laxatives over the counter without consulting a doctor. An occasional laxative probably causes little harm, but because of the unwanted effects described below, they should only be taken regularly under medical supervision. It is important to consult the doctor rather than take a laxative if the sluggishness of the bowels is a new or unusual problem, as occasionally this can be a symptom of an underlying serious disease. This is likely if the constipation is associated with vomiting, abdominal pain or bleeding from the back passage.

Before resorting to laxatives, other strategies are worth trying, such as including more fibre, fruit and fluids in the daily diet. Regular exercise can also help. Constipation is a common unwanted effect of various medicines, so it may be worth asking your doctor if yours could be contributing to your difficulties. If so, it may be possible to find an alternative.

The different types of laxatives are described below.

Bulk-forming laxatives (for example, bran in any form, ispaghula, sterculia, methyl celluose) These absorb water and produce a bigger, softer stool which is easier to pass.

Some preparations are distasteful to some people. They may cause excessive wind, but this is minimized if the dose is increased gradually. Rarely they may interfere with the absorption of some nutrients, and very rarely cause bowel blockage in people who have taken large amounts with very little fluid. This type of laxative is helpful in people who have hard stools, but less so in ill or frail people who have difficulty in passing soft stools.

Stimulant laxatives (for example, senna compounds, bisacodyl, sodium picosulphate) These increase bowel muscle action. They are usually taken at night and work the following morning.

Repeated use can cause excessive loss of fluids and potassium from the body and the failure of the normal pattern of bowel action. Short-term hazards include griping pain and an unpredictable response; a certain dose may produce diarrhoea in one person but be ineffective in another. Cascara and castor oil are very powerful stimulant laxatives whose effect is too strong; they are best avoided.

Stool softeners (for example, docusate) This is not very powerful but is occasionally useful in the short term, for instance after an operation for haemorrhoids.

Docusate can damage the bowel lining after prolonged use. The stool softener liquid paraffin should be avoided in the long term because of its unwanted effects. It can seep out of the back passage causing soiling, interfere with the absorption of vitamins, cause growths around the bowel and lead to pneumonia if it is regurgitated and inhaled.

'Osmotic' laxatives (for example, lactulose, Epsom salts, liver or health salts) These draw water into the bowel, producing a softer, easier-to-pass stool.

Lactulose is expensive, and sweet enough to nauseate some people, but is otherwise harmless. In the long term, 'salts' can cause dehydration and loss of potassium, or enough sodium retention to worsen heart failure. The occasional user runs a small risk, however.

Rectal preparations
Small enemas given by nurses, or glycerol (sometimes called glycerin) suppositories soften hard stools and lubricate their passage. Glycerol suppositories should be unwrapped, moistened

with water and pushed up the back passage end on; ask the doctor or nurse how to put them in if you do not know.

For the urinary system and genitals

For prostatic enlargement
Indoramin is sometimes used to relieve symptoms until an operation can be performed.

Unwanted effects include sleepiness, depression, dry mouth and nasal stuffiness, failure of ejaculation during intercourse and movement disorders.

Hormone replacement therapy (HRT) (using oestrogen plus a progestagen)

Short-term HRT This is used to relieve menopausal symptoms such as frequent hot flushes, emotional disorders such as depression, and the thinning and dryness of the vaginal lining which makes intercourse painful or difficult. Treatment is often stopped every six months or so and restarted only if symptoms recur.

Long-term HRT If given for ten to fifteen years after the menopause, HRT slows down the rate of bone-thinning (osteoporosis) and probably reduces the risk of a hip or wrist fracture in later life. Unfortunately it does not seem to strengthen the bones of women whose menopause occurred fifteen or more years ago. HRT may also protect women from heart and blood vessel disease, as their own hormones do during the childbearing years.

Among the unwanted effects of HRT is that oestrogen may encourage the growth of *existing* hormone-dependent cancers, so women who have had a breast, womb or ovarian cancer diagnosed are not usually given HRT. The risk of a *new* womb cancer developing can be abolished by giving a progestagen hormone for ten to twelve days a month, as well as the regular oestrogen compound. A woman whose womb has been removed (hysterectomy) does not of course need this. There is no evidence of an increased risk of breast cancer in women on HRT.

Other unwanted effects include breast tenderness and nausea. Bleeding from the uterus is usually brief and acceptable, but in some women may be painful and distressing.

Oestrogen administered by mouth produces very variable hormone levels in the body, so it is usually given in other ways. Implants under the skin are sometimes used, but the commonest method of administration is by adhesive patch impregnated with hormone. Patches must be used exactly as directed; they are usually reapplied every three to four days to keep the blood level of hormone approximately constant. Application below the waist rather than above seems to produce less breast tenderness. At present the progestagen component is taken by mouth, but it may shortly be possible to include it in a patch. Local vaginal creams or pessaries can be used for short-term treatment.

Evidence regarding the wise use and possible hazards of HRT is incomplete. Because of this, doctors have different views as to when – or, indeed, whether – HRT should be used. On balance, HRT seems to have more advantages than disadvantages for:

- women with troublesome menopausal symptoms;
- women at risk of osteoporosis (see page 74). It may become possible to identify those with low bone mass with a screening process. In the meantime white or Asian women approaching the menopause may want to read and think about HRT and discuss it with their doctors. Women with dark skins tend to have stronger bones and are less likely to need it.

The use of HRT is specialized, and research findings alter the details of its practice. It is therefore best supervised in a Menopause Clinic.

For diseases of the nervous system

For Parkinson's Disease

The drug treatment of Parkinson's Disease is based on the theory that normal functioning of the part of the brain concerned depends on a balance between two chemicals within it. One is called dopamine and the other, acetylcholine, has an opposite effect. As in Parkinson's the functioning of dopamine is reduced, the balance can be restored in one of two ways: either amounts of dopamine can be increased or amounts of acetylcholine reduced.

Levodopa This is given in a compound form, so that the dopamine is only released in the brain where its effect is wanted. This reduces the amount of unwanted effects due to the action of dopamine in the rest of the body.

The main benefit of levodopa is in improving mobility, although unfortunately it is less helpful in older people.

The amount and pattern of dosage is carefully tailored to the individual patient's needs, and it is vitally important that levodopa is taken exactly as prescribed. Mealtimes may need to be rearranged to help drug absorption. Vitamin supplements should not be taken without first checking with the doctor, as Vitamin B_6 (pyridoxine) interferes with the action of levodopa.

Unwanted effects include involuntary movements, restlessness, dizziness on standing upright with a tendency to fall over, mental confusion, nausea, vomiting and disturbances of heart rhythm. The effect on mobility can fluctuate, leading to tiresome 'on/off' and 'wearing off' reactions.

Amantidine This acts like levodopa and has few unwanted effects.

Bromocriptine This is similar but has long-lasting effects, so it is used to iron out 'wearing off' reactions to levodopa treatment.

Unwanted effects include mental confusion, nausea, vomiting and falls.

Selegiline This prolongs the action of levodopa so its dose can be reduced.

It may cause insomnia and psychiatric disturbances.

Anticholinergic drugs These block the action of acetylcholine and thus reduce its opposition to dopamine. This makes the most of what dopamine is available. Drugs used include benzhexol, procyclidine, orphenadrine, benztropine.

Unwanted effects include dry mouth, mental confusion, constipation, blurred vision with dilated pupils and difficulty in passing urine. Anticholinergics are unsuitable for people with glaucoma or prostatic enlargement.

Some Parkinsonian patients are helped by a beta-blocker to reduce tremor. Antidepressants and laxatives are prescribed as necessary.

For depression

Antidepressants (for example, the 'tricyclics', such as lofepramine, imipramine, amitryptyline)
These are prescribed for the more severe types of depression when general measures, psychotherapy and counselling are ineffective. They are taken in regular dosage, often once a day at bedtime to make best use of their sedative properties. The patient may sleep better within a day of starting treatment, but the improvement in mood can take two to four weeks.

The unwanted effects are the same as those of the anticholinergic drugs used for Parkinson's Disease described above.

Mianserin This is a newer drug which has fewer of these unwanted effects and is less dangerous in overdose. It is useful for people who are also being treated for high blood pressure, as it does not interfere with treatment as the tricyclic drugs do.

Occasionally mianserin causes serious blood abnormalities, so regular blood tests are necessary during treatment.

Antidepressant treatment is usually continued for at least six months after the patient is better and may go on indefinitely if this seems wise. It is also used to maintain the good effect of ECT.

Lithium This is most often used in bipolar depression, but is helpful in some other patients who have not responded to other drugs, and in preventing recurrence.

The unwanted effects of tremor, unsteadiness progressing to fits, and disturbance of thyroid and kidney function can be avoided if the blood level of the drug is checked frequently and the dose adjusted accordingly. Taking thiazide diuretics (see above) makes toxic effects more likely; they should not be taken by patients on lithium.

A severely depressed person may lack the motivation to take the tablets, and may also be contemplating suicide. It is therefore wise for a healthy person to take charge of medication and make sure the correct dose – no more, no less – is taken as directed.

For shingles

Anti-viral agents (for example, acyclovir, vidarabine)
These are sometimes given to patients with severe pain, those whose resistance is low because of other illness or medication, or who have severe complications. They have to be given as a seven-day course, starting as early as possible in the illness.

Unwanted effects include rashes, digestive upset, liver and blood disturbances, headache and tiredness.

Idoxuridine
Used as a local paint, it may shorten the period of pain, but to be effective it must be started as soon as the rash appears and be applied four times a day for four days.

Idoxuridine stings the skin and may damage it; food may taste different during treatment.

People with shingles often need painkillers, and some doctors think taking steroids makes the pain less likely to persist.

When shingles affects the eye (ophthalmic herpes), the patient will be prescribed special treatment by an eye specialist. This usually involves eye drops to rest the eye and others to reduce inflammation.

For sleep

Hypnotics (sedatives) (for example, loprazolam, temazepam, triazolam)
The tactics for coping with stress and using relaxation techniques described elsewhere (pages 27–8) should be tried before resorting

to medication. While it is reasonable to use hypnotics during a brief period of extra stress such as an illness, long-term use (say, more than three weeks) cannot be recommended.

Unwanted effects tend to be worse in an older person as the hypnotic drug builds up in the body. Even during a short period of use it is safer not to take a hypnotic every night. Mild and short-acting drugs like those named above are least harmful. Common problems include mental confusion, dizziness and incontinence; falls are less likely if the tablet is always taken after going to bed. Daytime sleepiness is often worse after a sleeping tablet than after a sleepless night, and it will be made worse by drinking alcohol or taking other sedative drugs such as those in some 'cold cures' and travel sickness medicines. Driving and using machinery is then best avoided. A person who has stopped taking sleeping tablets may experience 'rebound wakefulness' for a few nights before the body returns to normal.

For pain (analgesics)

Mild, household remedies (for example, paracetamol, aspirin)
These are often bought over the counter and used to treat headaches, muscle strain and mild joint problems. They are taken 'as required' and can be stopped when symptoms are not longer troublesome. Aspirin is more effective than paracetamol against inflammation and fever.

Paracetamol has few unwanted effects in normal use but is very dangerous in overdose; seek medical help *at once* for anyone who has taken excess paracetamol. Aspirin can irritate the stomach lining and cause bleeding which is occasionally severe. Ordinary aspirin is less irritant if taken after food, and 'buffered' preparations (such as aloxiprin) or enteric coated forms may be better tolerated.

On balance, paracetamol is probably the better choice as a household painkiller for a retired person. Proprietary compound preparations of paracetamol or aspirin cost more than plain

unbranded tablets and have few advantages; avoid the ones
containing codeine as it causes constipation.

Strong analgesics (narcotic analgesics or opioids, for example,
morphine, methadone, pethidine)
These are used for the short-term relief of acute pain, for example
after a heart attack or surgical operation, or in the longer term to
control pain in dying patients. The special expertise of a hospice
outreach team is often invaluable in making the end of life pain-
free and comfortable. In terminal care, painkillers are usually
given regularly according to an individually designed plan, so
that pain is not allowed to develop.

   Unwanted effects include nausea and constipation which may
require additional drug treatment. Cough is suppressed, breathing becomes shallower and there may be difficulty in passing
urine. Dependence may occur with all these medicines, which are
carefully controlled by law to stop them reaching the wrong
hands. Dependence is of no practical importance in dying people,
who should not be denied the pain relief they need because of a
false fear of 'addiction'.

For eye disease
Medicines given in the form of eye drops penetrate the eye
through the cornea. All eye preparations are issued sterile. They
can usually be safely used in the home for about a month, after
which any remainder should be discarded. It is wise to check the
package insert or ask the doctor or pharmacist how eye drops
should be stored. When two lots of eye drops are to be used, a few
minutes should be left after giving the first drops so that the
second lot do not wash them out before they have had time to act.
Ask for help from the GP or nurse if you have difficulty in coping
with eye drops or ointment; they may be able to show you useful
'tricks of the trade' and can arrange help if necessary.

For infections (antibiotics, for example, chloramphenicol,
neomycin)
Antibiotic eye drops often need to be applied frequently (every

two hours) during the day, with ointment at night to give a more prolonged effect during sleep.

For glaucoma

All the medicines described below need to be used regularly. If you find this difficult – for instance, if you have trouble putting in your eye drops – you should tell the doctor or nurse. If after some teaching you still cannot manage, a nurse will call to put the drops in.

Pilocarpine Used as eye drops, this acts to constrict the pupil and draw the muscular iris diaphragm inside the eye away from the fluid drainage channels. Pilocarpine is short acting, and is put in the eye three to six times a day.

It can cause blurred vision and brow ache.

Timolol This is a beta-blocking drug which probably acts by slowing the rate of production of eye fluids. It is used as eye drops.

Timolol may lead to dry eyes and allergy and if enough is absorbed into the bloodstream, causes the same unwanted effects as beta-blockers taken by mouth.

Acetazolamide This is swallowed as a tablet. It also seems to slow production of eye fluids.

In elderly people especially, acetazolamide can cause 'pins and needles' sensations, loss of body potassium, lack of appetite, sleepiness and depression.

For blood diseases

Anaemia

The cause of the anaemia should be found and treated if possible (see page 73). Other treatment depends on what is missing from the body. If you think you are anaemic it is wiser to consult the doctor than to buy a blood tonic over the counter. Tests are needed to identify the correct treatment, and treating blind (for example, if folate is given to someone with pernicious anaemia caused by B_{12} deficiency) can even be dangerous.

Iron This is taken by mouth whenever possible. It is given frequently, up to three times a day, until the anaemia is corrected, then continued for about three months to replace body iron stores.

Iron is sometimes given by intramuscular or intravenous injection to people who have had unacceptable unwanted effects with tablets or who cannot cooperate in taking them regularly.

With oral iron, unwanted effects include nausea, abdominal pain, constipation and diarrhoea. They are less common if the iron is taken after food or in a slow-release preparation, but this may be because the amount of iron absorbed is less. Intramuscular iron can stain the skin if not injected deeply enough and it very occasionally causes abnormalities of heart rhythm.

Vitamin B_{12} (hydroxocobalamin) This is given by intramuscular injection, as it is ineffective by mouth. Treatment starts intensively to replace body stores, with frequent injections every two to three days for about two weeks. After this the injections are repeated every three months for the rest of the patient's life.

No unwanted effects are known to occur.

Folic acid (folate) This is given by mouth for as long as necessary to correct the anaemia and replenish body stores. After this it can be stopped if the underlying cause of the deficiency can be removed.

Unwanted effects are few. Folic acid can cause fits in people taking phenytoin to control epilepsy, as it reduces the concentration of phenytoin in the blood. Some cancers grow faster with folate, so its use is avoided in patients known to have them. It does *not* cause cancer itself.

For bones, joints and muscles

Osteoporosis

(a) Prevention Hormone replacement therapy (HRT) is the most effective preventative measure (see pages 118–19).

Calcium supplements may help in people whose dietary intake

is unsatisfactory. Other treatments are currently being tried in women who are unsuitable for HRT; these include fluoride, calcitonin and diphosphonates.

Calcium supplements can cause constipation and flatulence; they should not be taken by people with kidney disease.

(b) Treatment once present We do not know whether reversal of established osteoporosis is possible, but it seems sensible to make sure dietary calcium intake is adequate and to provide supplements if it is not.

Paget's Disease
Many patients require only pain relief. Others need treatment to slow down the over-active formation and absorption of bone. Two types are used:

Calcitonin This is a hormone produced by the thyroid glands of various animals including humans. It is used in people whose Paget's Disease is causing severe pain or deformity, or when abnormal bone is pressing on other tissues. It is given by injection about three times a week or more often if necessary, for three to six months or longer.

Unwanted effects include nausea, vomiting and flushing of the hands and face. They are not usually severe enough for treatment to be stopped.

Disodium etidronate (EHDP) This is an alternative which can be given orally in courses of three to six months. If used for longer than this the bones may become thin and break easily. Taking food within two hours of the dose can interfere with its action.

It can cause nausea, diarrhoea and a metallic taste in the mouth.

Osteoarthritis
Painkillers such as paracetamol may be sufficient to relieve symptoms in milder cases.

NSAIDs (non-steroidal anti-inflammatory drugs, for example benorylate, ibuprofen and naproxen) These are used in more severe arthritis and also help other conditions of the bones, joints and surrounding tissues, such as 'frozen shoulder', (see page 79), neck pain and backache. Taken regularly by mouth, they relieve pain and also damp down inflammation.

NSAIDs can cause digestive upset of any degree, ranging from mild pain through more severe symptoms of pain, nausea, vomiting and diarrhoea to serious bleeding from the gut. NSAIDs are not usually given to people with acute gastric or duodenal ulcers. People with a healed ulcer may take an NSAID with an acid-reducing drug such as ranitidine to reduce the risk of the ulcer reopening. NSAIDs should always be taken with food or milk, and digestive symptoms while taking them should be reported to the doctor promptly.

It is often difficult to decide whether the good effects of an NSAID outweigh the risk of unwanted effects, and you may wish to discuss this with your doctor.

Gout

Acute attacks These are treated with NSAIDs. Indomethacin taken by mouth in reducing doses may be used, providing treatment takes less than a week.

Unwanted effects of headache, drowsiness, dizziness and digestive upsets occur, but are rare in such short courses.

Chronic treatment This is needed for patients with a persisting high level of urate in their blood. It should only be started under 'cover' from an NSAID or small doses of colchicine, as otherwise an acute attack of gout may be precipitated. Suitable medicines include *allopurinol*, which slows the formation of urate and is especially useful in patients with damaged kidneys. *Probenicid* and *sulphinpyrazone* help the kidneys to get rid of urate and are only suitable for patients with good kidney function, who need to drink plenty of fluids to help flush out the urate and prevent it forming kidney stones.

Unwanted effects are rare, although allopurinol may cause skin rashes.

The glands

Thyroid disease

Under-activity of the gland This is treated by replacement of the missing thyroid hormone *thyroxine*. The dose is increased gradually to the correct maintenance amount. This can be taken as a single daily dose by mouth, preferably before breakfast. Once started it is continued for life.

Thyroxine can cause irregularities of the heartbeat, angina, headache, restlessness, weight loss, flushing and diarrhoea. It has to be used carefully in patients with heart disease.

Over-activity of the gland This is controlled by anti-thyroid medicines e.g. *carbimazole*. These interfere with the manufacture of thyroid hormones inside the gland. Carbimazole can also be used to damp down an over-active thyroid before surgery or radio-iodine.

The commonest unwanted effect is an itchy rash. This can either be treated with antihistamines, or *propylthiouracil* may be substituted for carbimazole. More seriously but much more rarely, white blood cell production may be suppressed. This may cause a sore throat, so patients taking carbimazole are told to report such symptoms promptly to the doctor.

The beta-blocker *propranolol* is occasionally given together with carbimazole or propylthiouracil when the over-active thyroid is causing irregularities of heart rhythm.

Diabetes

Some older people with diabetes have to follow a diet but need no other treatment. Between a third and a half of older patients need tablets (oral hypoglycaemic agents or OHAs). A few need insulin injections.

Two types of OHAs are used: sulphonylureas and biguanides.

Sulphonylureas (for example, tolbutamide, gliclazide, glipizide) These stimulate the pancreas to produce more insulin and probably act to lower blood sugar elsewhere in the body.

The most important unwanted effect is hypoglycaemia, a dangerous lowering of blood sugar below the normal level. The early signs of this are drowsiness, irritability and mental confusion, which may be less obvious to the hypoglycaemic diabetic than to a companion. If not treated, hypoglycaemia can cause coma and even death. Patients taking OHAs can become hypoglycaemic if:

- the dose of the OHA is too large – for example, if a second tablet is taken by mistake.
- there is insufficient sugar from food in the body to 'mop up' the effect of the tablet – for example, if a meal is missed. The evening meal is a particularly dangerous one to omit, as nocturnal hypoglycaemia may not be noticed in time.
- other drugs are taken which increase the action of OHAs, such as aspirin, some NSAIDs and some antibiotics. People taking OHAs should carry details of their medication to show to any new doctor who may treat them.

Other unwanted effects are uncommon and less serious. They include digestive upsets, rashes and jaundice.

Biguanides (for example, metformin) This slows down the body's manufacture of glucose while increasing the ability to use it up. It tends to depress the appetite, so is useful in people who need to lose weight.

The unwanted effects of dyspepsia, nausea and vomiting are less likely if the dose is increased gradually and the tablets taken with food. Metformin cannot be used in people with impaired kidney function because of the risk of a severe metabolic abnormality called lactic acidosis; heavy drinkers are particularly vulnerable to this.

People who have been taking metformin for a long time may fail to absorb nutrients like vitamin B_{12} properly.

Insulin An older person whose diabetes is usually controlled by diet or tablets may need insulin injections for a short while during an acute illness or surgical operation. Few older diabetics need insulin injections all the time. Those who do usually take a single morning dose. Patients with sufficiently good sight and dexterity can give their own, while others will be visited by a nurse.

The main unwanted effect is hypoglycaemia, caused by too much insulin or too little food. Skin complications such as infection and changes in fat contour can occur at the injection site.

Steroids

Steroid hormones are produced naturally in the healthy body and are essential to life. Extra amounts are given as medicine for conditions such as giant cell (temporal) arteritis, asthma and wheezy bronchitis, and some skin and eye diseases. Although the benefits of steroids can be great, their use can be hazardous, so the minimum effective dose is used for the shortest possible time. Whenever possible steroids are given locally – for example, as inhalations for lung disease, or as skin creams and eye drops. This gives the maximum treatment benefit for the minimum general effect. Although in serious illnesses steroids can be given by injection, they are also effective as tablets taken by mouth.

The unwanted effects depend on the size of the dose, the length of time for which it is given and the route of administration.

Steroids by mouth

High doses can cause mental disturbances such as confusion. Heart failure and a rise in blood pressure can happen because steroids make the body retain salt and water. Diabetes is made worse, and it can be brought on in people who are predisposed to it. Long-term treatment causes osteoporosis (bone-thinning), with squashing of a vertebra and a tendency to break bones. Peptic ulcers can occur and these may bleed or perforate.

When steroids are given as medicine, the body's own steroid production tends to switch off. If the steroid treatment is suddenly stopped or if the need for steroids suddenly rises because of illness or other stress, the body will not be able to compensate by increasing its own steroid production in the usual way. It is therefore very important to increase the dose of steroids at times of increased need, and it is *very dangerous* to stop steroid treatment suddenly. When the dose is decreased or treatment stopped altogether, this is always done gradually to give the body a chance to take over steroid production again.

If you are prescribed steroid tablets, you will be given a card to carry giving details of your treatment. You will find it useful to show this to any new doctor, nurse or pharmacist you meet, especially to an anaesthetist visiting you before an operation.

Always make sure you have a reserve supply of steroids so that you do not run out. Let the doctor know if you become ill as your steroid dose may need to be increased. This is especially import-ant if vomiting or diarrhoea is interfering with your treatment; you may need injections instead.

If you develop indigestion symptoms you should report to the doctor at once in case they are an early sign of a peptic ulcer.

Steroid skin creams
These should not be used on infected skin, as the steroid damps down the inflammatory reaction that normally restrains infection. To prevent thinning and other changes in the skin, the weakest possible preparation should be used for the shortest possible time.

A steroid cream now be bought over the counter. Small quantities can be safely rubbed into an affected area once or twice a day for seven days. The cream should be kept away from broken or infected skin, and the doctor consulted if symptoms persist after a week's treatment.

Steroid eye drops
These should *never* be used without a doctor's approval, as they can conceal the danger signs of serious conditions until it is too late. They can also bring on glaucoma in susceptible people.

Antibiotics

This is the name doctors and pharmacists use for medicines to treat infections, whether by bacteria, fungi or viruses – antibacterials, antifungals and antiviral agents respectively.

Antibacterials (for example, penicillin, amoxycillin, cotrimoxazole)

These are what most people refer to as 'antibiotics'. They kill bacteria, but not viruses such as those responsible for colds and 'flu. When given by mouth, they need to be taken several times a day so that the level of antibacterial in the blood is sufficient to oppose the bacteria at all times. Do not alter the dose or timing of your antibacterial without first checking with the doctor. Antibacterials are usually given as a course over a number of days so as to eliminate all bacteria from the body. It may be tempting to stop taking the medicine before the end of the course if you feel better. This is a mistake, as lurking germs may break out again. This time the infection will be more difficult to treat, as the germs will have become resistant to the medicine.

The choice of antibacterial depends partly on the likely cause of the illness. To find out which germ is responsible and thus which medicine will get rid of it, the doctor may take a specimen, for example of the patient's urine, from which the germ may be grown in the laboratory. This takes at least forty-eight hours, but once the result is available, treatment started after the specimen was taken may be altered if necessary. The right choice of medicine also depends on the patient's age and general state of health.

Unwanted effects include allergies, especially to penicillin, nausea, diarrhoea, skin rashes, fever, joint pains and thrush. Tell the doctor at once if you think an antibacterial is upsetting you, and make sure he knows about it if one has done so in the past.

Antibacterials are sometimes used as local applications, for example in ointments or drops for eye infections. This can be a useful way of killing the germs responsible without enough medicine getting into the body to cause unwanted effects.

Antibacterials are not often applied directly to the skin as they tend to cause sensitivity reactions.

Antifungal drugs

Thrush is a fungal infection, causing a sore mouth with white patches, or itching and soreness of the vagina and genital area. Fungal infections of the skin are also quite common. Local applications are usually sufficient for these infections, for example *Nystatin* pastilles or suspension for oral thrush.

Fungi can cause severe infections in people whose resistance is low, perhaps because of other illnesses. These usually need hospital treatment.

Antiviral agents

In general these are less useful and effective than the antibacterials. Fortunately, many viral infections, like colds and 'flu, get better on their own. *Acyclovir* and *idoxuridine* are occasionally used against herpes viruses (see Shingles, pages 63 and 122).

Anti-cancer drugs

Two sorts of drugs are used to halt the growth of cancer cells: cytotoxic drugs and hormones. They act on both the primary cancer and any secondary deposits.

Cytotoxic drugs

These poison cancer cells by interfering with their growth or metabolism in various ways. Not all types of cancer are susceptible to their effects. They have been particularly successful in treating leukaemias and lymphomas (tumours of lymph gland tissue). They are less often used for solid tumours like those of the lung or breast. When fluid accumulates in body cavities because of cancer, cytotoxic drugs are sometimes injected into the cavity after the fluid has been drained off, to prevent it from coming back.

Unwanted effects occur because it is unfortunately not

possible to confine the actions of cytotoxics to the undesirable
cancer cells. Common consequences of the partial poisoning of
normal cells include:

- Pain and tissue damage if a cytotoxic being injected into a vein
  accidentally leaks outside it.
- Sickness and vomiting; this can often be forestalled by careful
  treatment.
- Suppression of the bone marrow cells that produce blood cells
  to fight infection, so the patient's resistance is lowered. He or
  she is asked to report any feverish illness at once so that it can
  be treated promptly. In addition, regular blood counts are
  performed, so the cytotoxics can be stopped for a time to allow
  the bone marrow to recover if this seems necessary.
- Loss of hair. Nothing can be done to prevent this, but the hair
  usually grows back again rapidly once treatment is stopped.

All cytotoxics can cause the above ill-effects. In addition, particular drugs have their individual drawbacks.

Cyclophosphamide Used for chronic lymphocytic leukaemia. It
can cause a severe inflammation of the bladder, but this can be
prevented by the protective drug *mesna* and by drinking plenty of
fluids.

Busulphan Used for chronic myeloid leukaemia. It pigments the
skin, especially in creases.

Vincristine Used for various cancers. It can cause nerve damage,
which results in 'pins and needles', loss of reflexes and sometimes
interference with bowel, bladder or sexual function.

Prescribing cytotoxics for maximum benefit and minimum harm
takes special knowledge and experience. Treatment is usually
supervised by a specialist, often a medical oncologist. Some drugs
are given in hospital, others on an outpatient basis. It is obviously
important that the patient knows what to expect and in particular
what unwanted effects to report.

Hormone therapy for cancer
Cancer of the breast or prostate may respond to hormone therapy. Treatment involves either blocking the action of the growth-promoting hormone, or using one with the opposite effect.

Breast cancer Tamoxifen opposes the action of the female hormone oestrogen. Unwanted effects are uncommon. Patients whose cancer has spread to the bones may get a worsening of their pain before the deposits start to shrink.

Aminoglutethimide is similar. Steroid replacement has to be given with it. Unwanted effects include drowsiness, fever and rashes, which soon get better.

Prostatic cancer This tumour needs the male hormone testosterone in order to grow. One way of depriving the cancer of testosterone is to remove both testicles surgically. Various drugs can give the same effect.

Unwanted effects are impotence, shrinkage of genitals and enlargement of breasts, which may get better if and when the treatment is stopped. Nausea, abnormal blood clotting, fluid retention and liver disturbance may occur with *diethylstilboestrol* (DES), a synthetic oestrogen, but are less common with *cyproterone acetate* (CPA). Both these medicines come as tablets which need to be taken regularly. *Goserelin* can be given as a depot injection under the skin of the abdominal wall every twenty-eight days. *Buserelin* is given three times a day for a week as an injection but can be taken as a nasal spray thereafter.

Vitamins
Healthy people, elderly or not, can get all the vitamins they need from a balanced diet. Taking extra vitamins is unnecessary, expensive and can be dangerous. When the diet is poor, it is better to try and improve it rather than to resort to vitamin supplements.

The situation is different for two groups of *sick* people: those who have difficulty in absorbing vitamins and other nutrients from food, and those whose vitamin requirements are higher than normal. People in these groups may need extra vitamins as medicine.

Vitamin A

Deficiency can occur in people who cannot absorb dietary fat. They develop eye changes, especially night blindness, and have an increased tendency to tracheitis, bronchitis and pneumonia.

Excessive Vitamin A causes liver and bone damage and skin changes; it can be fatal.

Vitamin B group

Thiamine (Vitamin B_1) deficiency occurs in some alcoholics, and failure to absorb Vitamin B_{12} causes pernicious anaemia (see Anaemia, pages 72–3 and 125–6). Otherwise, only severely malnourished people lack B vitamins.

Unwanted effects are few. Pyridoxine (Vitamin B_6) causes nerve damage in large doses. It can also interfere with the action of levodopa used for Parkinson's Disease (see page 120).

Vitamin C (ascorbic acid)

Dietary lack is quite common in elderly people taking poor diets, especially those living in institutions. Whenever possible the deficiency should be made up by fruit or fruit juice, with ascorbic acid tablets as a last resort. Injured people and those recovering from surgical operations may benefit from extra Vitamin C, which helps healing. There is little evidence that 'megadoses' of Vitamin C benefit health in any way.

Large doses cause diarrhoea and other digestive upsets and may contribute to the formation of some kidney stones.

Vitamin D

Supplements may be needed by housebound elderly people whose diet is inadequate and who lack the chance to manufacture Vitamin D in the skin on exposure to sunlight. The extra Vitamin D can be taken by mouth, or given as injections to people who find it difficult to take tablets regularly. Other people needing supplements include those with food absorption problems and those taking tablets to prevent epilepsy.

The most important unwanted effect is kidney damage from raised blood calcium, but nausea, vomiting, abdominal pain and mental changes also occur.

Vitamin K
Injections of this vitamin may be needed by people who cannot absorb it from food.

Vitamin K has the effect of opposing the action of some anticoagulant drugs.

4

Getting Help

Help with health and welfare difficulties is available from a number of statutory and voluntary services, described in this chapter. What is on offer and how much it costs varies a lot around the country. Who does what – which duty falls to which service – also differs from place to place. It is therefore very important to know your patch.

To find out what is available in your area, you may want to approach the secretary of your local Community Health Council, visit the Citizens' Advice Bureau, ask at the Town Hall or Public Library or get in touch with your local branch of Age Concern. It is worth remembering that services are demand-led; if you identify an unmet need, you may want to press for it to be met.

Because many recently retired people are caring for much older relatives or friends, information useful to frail people has been included. Please do not feel patronized if some suggestions seem obvious; they are included because simple measures are easily overlooked by preoccupied, tired carers who are under pressure.

Health services

The general practitioner (also called a family practitioner)

What he/she does
The GP is of course responsible for attending to your day-to-day health needs, treating you when you are ill and providing

preventative services like health screening and immunization. He or she can also refer patients to other members of the primary health care team, such as the district nurse or health visitor. The GP may work single-handed or, more commonly, with other doctors as a group practice in a health centre, when other services such as chiropody or dentistry may be available under the same roof. As he or she cannot always be on duty, arrangements have to be made for out-of-hours cover at night and over weekends and public holidays. Some group practices are large enough to organize their own on-call rota; this means that if you become ill out of hours you will see one of the doctors who work in the practice and whom you may well already know. In other areas a doctor from a deputizing service will be on call. You should always be able to leave messages for your doctor or his deputy. The usual surgery telephone number should refer you to whoever is on call.

GPs provide access to other medical services, such as specialist hospital clinics. It is not usually possible to see a specialist without a referral letter from your GP. This is in the patient's interests for two reasons. First, a certain amount of medical knowledge may be necessary to decide which sort of specialist is needed, and delay or misunderstandings may follow if the wrong sort of doctor is consulted first. Second, the GP knows the whole of the patient's medical background, and can make sure that hospital specialists are given adequate general information on which to base their opinions, and that the treatment they prescribe is compatible with that already being given.

You have a right to see a doctor (not necessarily your own GP) at the surgery during surgery hours. If you have not made an appointment, you may be offered one at a later surgery. If you think your problem will not wait you should say so politely but firmly. The GP is not necessarily obliged to visit patients at home, but is allowed to use his or her own judgement as to whether this is necessary. If you think you need a visit but the receptionist is reluctant to arrange one, you can ask to discuss the matter with the doctor directly, as it is a medical decision. You should be prepared to ring back at a prearranged time when the doctor is free to take these calls.

Choosing a GP
Everyone is entitled to be on the list of a family doctor, and it is wise to get this done before becoming ill, as the choice can then be more leisurely. You can obtain a list of local doctors providing NHS treatment from main post offices, some police stations and libraries or directly from the Family Health Services Authority (formerly Family Practitioner Committee) (address under 'F' in the Business and Services section of the telephone book). Your local Community Health Council can help with addresses and also with the rather complicated administrative procedures described below. (The CHC's address will be under the name of the Health Authority in the telephone book and also under 'C').

It is worth giving a little thought to what you expect of your doctor and his or her practice. For instance, do you prefer a doctor of your own sex or of a particular age? What sort of personality are you most comfortable with? What are the practice deputizing arrangements? What other services are available 'on site'?

The next task is to find the information. Asking round among neighbours and friends is a good way of finding out about the more nebulous qualities of style and personality. A few practices encourage prospective patients to visit the surgery and talk to the doctor before deciding to join his or her list. You can call at the surgery or health centre to find out about the range of services on offer, and also whether the surgery hours and arrangements fit in with your life; there may be a 'first come, first served' system, an appointments system or a mixture of both. Practices now produce a leaflet containing all this information.

It is difficult for a layman to assess a doctor's professional qualifications, though a word with a doctor friend may be useful. If a doctor has the letters 'DGM' after his or her name, he or she holds the Diploma in Geriatric Medicine. This means that he or she has studied the health needs of older people, and is likely to be especially sympathetic to their problems.

Getting on a doctor's list

This procedure is used when you have moved house and changed your address. Having identified the doctor you prefer, the next step is to ask at the surgery whether Dr X has space on his/her list and is willing to accept you. If so, you then need to fill in the appropriate section of your medical card and give it to your doctor to sign. The surgery staff then send the card to the FHSA for registration, and the FHSA will send you a new medical card. They will also replace lost cards.

Good doctors, not surprisingly, tend to be popular, and you may find your first choice has no vacancies. Though this is disappointing, it is an inevitable part of the current system. It would obviously be unwise for a popular doctor to take on more patients than could reasonably be coped with, as the standard of care would then fall.

If after several attempts you are still unable to find a doctor who will accept you, you should write to the Family Health Services Authority who will find a doctor for you.

If you change your address and do not wish to change your doctor, you should ask him or her whether he or she is still willing to undertake your care. If you are living outside the practice area the doctor is entitled to refuse, while if still willing to look after you, the doctor will need to tell the FHSA.

Changing your doctor when you have not moved house

The procedure for this is slightly different. You may want to make certain the new doctor will accept you before you leave the old one. If you wish you can ask for your old doctor's consent to the change. When the doctor has given this, he or she signs Part B of the medical card, you complete Part B and then give your card to your new doctor, who sends it on to the FHSA. The FHSA will then send you a new card.

You may prefer not to seek your present doctor's consent, or he may have refused to release you. In these circumstances you can send your medical card to the FHSA with a letter saying that you wish to change doctors. The card will be returned with a slip attached, allowing you to find a new doctor within a month; after this has elapsed you will need to apply again.

In some places it may be difficult to find a new doctor who will accept you. In an emergency you are entitled to treatment from any available doctor in the district. For long-term treatment you should write to the FHSA, asking them to find a doctor for you. In your letter you should tell the FHSA which doctors have refused you and also which doctors you would prefer not to be registered with.

A GP may remove any patient from his or her list without giving a reason. He or she has to tell the FHSA, who will then let the patient know. The FHSA must make sure that you are not left without a doctor.

Using your doctor

On the whole it is more important to report early when you notice something wrong with your body rather than to rely on a health check to pick up faults. (Important symptoms which should be reported early are noted on pages 35–6.) If you sometimes feel reluctant to 'trouble' the doctor, it helps to remember that you are still paying him or her.

You cannot of course be examined by a doctor without your consent, though if you ask his or her advice you are usually assumed to have consented to medical examination. You are entitled to decide whether or not to accept any treatment that is offered to you; make sure you discuss the options with your doctor and express your preference.

Having chosen a doctor you think you will find easy to talk to, try to be as open as possible. Tell him or her if you are worried that a seemingly trivial symptom may indicate a serious illness; he or she will probably be able to reassure you that your fears are groundless. It is also important to speak up if you have stopped taking a prescribed medicine for any reason or if you are taking one you have bought over the counter. If you have been consulting an alternative practitioner, it is also wise to say so. If your doctor is not fully informed on these matters, he or she may unwittingly harm your health with an unsuitable or incompatible treatment.

It is often difficult for a doctor to know how much to tell patients about their condition, especially at an early stage when a number of possibilities are being considered. In general it seems that patients want to know more now, and doctors explain more accordingly, but this is not always the case: some doctors tend to keep things to themselves, while some patients prefer to be protected from bad news. Do not be afraid to ask for more information: you have a right to know what is happening to your body, and doctors should answer your questions fully and truthfully when they concern your own health.

However, doctors have a strict duty to preserve their patients' privacy, except when compelled to give information to an authority such as a court. They will only pass confidential information to other professionals concerned in your care, such as nurses, dietitians, physiotherapists or other doctors, or in some cases, to your close relatives. You should tell your doctor if there is something about your health you would prefer your relatives not to know.

Doctors tend to be under considerable pressure during surgery times, and the atmosphere may not be suitable for a quiet discussion. In the rush it is easy for important matters to get forgotten; it can help to list the important topics you wish covered. If your doctor is very busy, you can ask when you can come back to discuss things at more leisure.

Emergencies

It is obviously best to consult your doctor during normal working hours whenever possible. Not only will he or she be less tired and rushed than in the middle of the night, but back-up services such as x-ray and laboratories will be fully staffed. However, illness is no respecter of clock or calendar and people can and do need medical help at 'unsocial' hours. Sometimes this is quite unavoidable, but in other cases the 'emergency' can be avoided with forethought: for instance, someone who is unwell in the week

before a public holiday such as Christmas or Easter should seek
help in good time, rather than waiting to see what happens.

Emergency calls should be made to your doctor's usual
telephone number in the first instance. '999' calls should be
reserved for urgent cases when perhaps the doctor is out on a call
and is not immediately available. Try not to use hospital Accident
and Emergency Departments for routine health problems as this
can cause delays in the treatment of seriously ill or injured people.

If you need to see a doctor when you are away from home –
for example when on holiday or staying with family or friends
– a GP can accept you as a temporary patient. If he or she does
not wish to do this, you must still be given any treatment you
need right away.

In hospital

Many hospitals produce an information booklet which is sent to
prospective patients. If your admission is a routine, arranged one,
you will have time to read this before you go in.

As a hospital patient, you are entitled to full information about
your condition, its treatment and the outlook for the future. If
you find it difficult to ask questions during the ward round, you
can ask the ward sister to arrange for you to see the doctor
privately at another time.

If you have an operation, you will be asked to sign a consent
form beforehand. This is a good opportunity to make sure you
understand why the operation is necessary and what its effects
will be – for instance, whether it will leave you with a stoma or
may affect your sex life. If your operation is exploratory – for
instance, a biopsy of a lump – you should discuss the likely extent
of the procedure with the surgeon; some people like all necessary
treatment to be got over under the same anaesthetic, while others
like to wake up and discuss future possibilities before giving
consent to a major procedure.

Medical students gain experience in the wards and outpatient
departments of teaching hospitals by talking with patients and
learning to examine them; this is very helpful to the doctors – and

patients – of the future. You do not of course have to be seen by students; if you prefer not to, you should tell the nurse in charge.

You are free to refuse any sort of treatment and can of course leave the hospital at any time, though you may be asked to sign a form stating that you did this against medical advice.

When things go wrong – how to complain

All human relationships have their ups and downs; those between doctors and patients are not exceptions. It may help to remember that there is nothing special about doctors. We are just ordinary human beings whose education and experience enable us to advise people about their health and treat them when they are ill. We have no special moral or personal qualities that make us necessarily more unselfish, patient or kind than anyone else. We are no better at coping with unhappiness, whether in our personal lives or among our patients. Being fallible, we make mistakes and worry about making more. Sometimes these stresses – perhaps aggravated by lack of sleep – can make even the best of us irritable and less sympathetic than we should be. In addition, the chronic underfunding and understaffing of the NHS means there is never enough time.

Knowing all this may make it easier for you to keep your head and your temper if and when a doctor who is usually pleasant and helpful is uncharacteristically snappish or uncooperative. Normal friendly relations are most likely to be restored if you make as little as possible of an isolated incident of this sort, rather than by retaliating or taking offence. There are, however, no excuses for callousness, persistent rudeness, incompetence or negligence. If you meet any of these, you are fully justified in making a complaint and should do so.

A family doctor's terms of service oblige him or her to work in a certain way and breaches of these terms can be investigated by the Family Health Services Authority. In addition the General Medical Council imposes certain ethical and professional standards on all doctors, as does a similar council on nurses, midwives and health visitors. Many people, both patients and doctors, find the current complaints procedure cumbersome and unsatisfactory, and there is some hope of change in the near future. In the meantime, the best course of action for a dissatisfied patient is to talk with the doctor, dentist, nurse or whoever is concerned, him or herself, to try and put things right; older patients with their long experience of dealing with people are often very skilled at this.

In hospital it is also best to start with a direct approach. If this is difficult or unsuccessful, there should be a senior staff member available to help with your complaint.

If you are still not satisfied, it is best to get in touch with the secretary of the Community Health Council, who can advise on the next step. CHC staff can either represent a patient informally to a family doctor or hospital consultant, or if necessary can help with the formal complaints procedure. Prompt action is advisable, while details are fresh in the minds of all concerned; late complaints may not be allowed.

A useful leaflet, *Patients' rights – a summary of your rights and responsibilities in the NHS,* is available from Community Health Councils (see page 153).

Nurses

District or community nurses and practice nurses

The district or community nurse is usually attached to the GP's practice and can be seen at the surgery or health centre, or be reached by a telephone call to the receptionist or practice manager. Some doctors also employ their own practice nurse. In some practices you can see a nurse directly yourself, while in others the doctor sees patients first.

Nurses are playing an increasing part in preventative health care such as screening and in the monitoring of long-standing conditions such as diabetes and high blood pressure. They also undertake treatment such as wound care and ear syringeing. Nurses may visit patients at home to change catheters or dressings or to give injections. They acquire great expertise in the practical aspects of chronic illnesses and can teach valuable nursing skills to relatives and other carers. The nurse based at the surgery is likely to know whether the specialist nurses described below work in your area and if so, where they may be found.

Community psychiatric nurses (CPNs)
These have special experience of mental health nursing. They monitor the progress outside hospital of people of any age who are suffering from a mental illness, and also care for elderly confused people. Community psychiatric nurses have practical experience of day-to-day problems which makes them valuable sources of advice and help, for instance to the relatives, friends and neighbours of an old person who wanders, neglects herself or causes a disturbance. CPNs may be based at health centres, psychogeriatric hospitals or at the headquarters of a Community Mental Health Care team; the GP's receptionist, the community nurse, the health visitor or the secretary of the Community Health Council should know where one can be found.

Geriatric liaison nurse
You may come across a geriatric liaison nurse if you or someone you know are admitted to a hospital geriatric department. She or he is a community nurse who goes between the hospital and the outside world and helps to ensure the patient is fit and independent enough to go home. After home discharge the nurse will monitor the patient for a short while so that a rapid return to hospital can be arranged if things go wrong.

Night nursing and respite care
In some areas there is a special team of community 'twilight nurses'. These give late evening treatment and help patients into bed for the night. The district nurse will know whether or not a twilight service is available.

Night sitting to relieve someone caring for a frail or unwell dependant can sometimes be arranged, for example through a Crossroads Care Attendant Scheme (see pages 28 and 168) or the

Red Cross; the community nurse, local Social Services Department or branch of Age Concern will be able to give you information on what is available in your area. Private nurses can of course be obtained from agencies, but private nursing can be expensive.

Respite care during the day or for a longer break to give a carer a holiday may be available in a hospital, old people's home or other place as appropriate. The doctor or nurse will be able to advise about this.

Cancer nurses

Some nurses have special training in providing symptom relief and the sort of continuing care that helps a cancer sufferer who wishes to do so to remain at home for as long as possible. Both the National Society for Cancer Relief (Macmillan Fund) and the Marie Curie Foundation operate a community nursing service and run homes for respite care; the GP and the community nurse have access to these services. Home care is also provided by outreach teams from hospices; contact the Hospice Information Service for further details (see page 169).

Continence advisers

These nurses have special training and experience in normal and abnormal bladder and bowel function. Continence advisers work in special Continence Clinics and visit patients in their own homes, where they can give individually tailored advice.

Not all health authorities employ a continence adviser. Your GP or the district nurse may know if there is one based near you. Alternatively, the Association of Continence Advisers (see page 168) has information on services round the country.

If incontinence persists despite treatment, equipment such as pads and pants may be available cheaply or even free from the local Health Authority; the nurse or GP will know about this. Some Social Services Departments run an Incontinence Laundry Service to help with soiled linen, and the occupational therapist may be able to suggest modifications such as grab-rails or a raised seat which will make the lavatory easier to use. The occupational therapist is based at Social Services. Equipment such as commodes can sometimes be borrowed from the Red Cross, St John's Ambulance or WRVS.

A fact sheet entitled *Help with Incontinence* is available from Age Concern England (see page 167).

Stoma care nurses
These work both in hospital and in the community, giving practical advice and emotional support before and after the operation that creates the stoma. If you are a stoma patient you will be put in touch with a stoma care nurse while you are in hospital. If you subsequently move or lose touch with your stoma care nurse, the district nurse will know where she or he can be reached.

Health visitors
A health visitor is a nurse who has had an extra year's training in preventative medicine, psychology, public health and sociology. She usually works as part of the primary health care team and can be reached at the doctor's surgery or health centre.

Health visitors have proved to be particularly successful in checking on the general well-being of older patients and ensuring they are offered whatever social, financial or medical help they need to maintain health and independence. Unfortunately they are in short supply and tend to work mainly with families with small children.

Physiotherapists
'Physios' specialize in movement and its disorders. Their work strengthens weak muscles, loosens stiff joints, and helps people with disabling illness such as stroke or Parkinson's Disease to become as independent as possible.

Physios work in hospitals, including day hospitals, and increasingly are reaching out into the community from health centres to treat patients at home.

When NHS physiotherapy is in short supply, it is possible to pay to see a physio privately. It is wise to ask the doctor whether this is appropriate, and if so to ask him to write a referral letter. The physio should be state-registered and a member of the Chartered Society of Physiotherapy, with the letters 'SRP, MCSP' after his or her name.

Dentists

Finding a dentist

From October 1990 patients register with a dentist for continuing care, as they do with a family doctor. Once you are registered with him or her, the dentist will either treat you under the NHS personally, or may sub-contract part of the work to another dentist. The contract with your dentist lapses after two years from the last treatment, but if, as is sensible, you attend more often, it is renewed automatically at the end of each course. The arrangements for changing your dentist are similar to those for changing your doctor.

After examining you at your first and subsequent visits, your dentist will give you a treatment plan. This will describe each part of your treatment and specify its cost. Your plan may include both NHS and private treatment in the same course, but the NHS will not contribute to the cost of private treatment.

A dentist does not have to take on anyone who asks for treatment, and in some areas you may have difficulty in finding one. In this case you would get in touch with the Family Health Services Authority (formerly Family Practitioner Committee), the Community Health Council, Citizens' Advice Bureau or branch of Age Concern, or the District Dental Officer of the local Community Dental Service, reached via the Health Authority.

If you have difficulty getting to the dentist's surgery

Some dentists may visit older people to treat them at home, or the Community Dental Service may operate a home care system; ask at the Community Health Council. Alternatively, your local branch of Age Concern may be able to advise about special transport, for instance a local branch of a Dial-a-Ride service.

Emergency dental treatment

If you have severe toothache, bleeding from a gum or a similar problem, you should get in touch with your dentist at his usual telephone number. If he or she is not able to treat you him- or herself, you will be directed to a dentist who can provide urgent care.

As these arrangements are new, it may be a little while before they are operating smoothly. Practice information leaflets should be available at the dentist's surgery, and the Family Health Services Authority will provide information or help with any difficulties.

Chiropodists

These can diagnose and treat all foot disorders and also know about general illnesses that affect the feet, such as diabetes and circulatory diseases.

Chiropodists see patients either on the NHS or privately. It is best to seek one whose qualifications are sufficient for state registration and who therefore has the letters 'SRCh' after his or her name.

It is usually possible to refer yourself to a chiropodist without a doctor's letter. However, chiropody may be available at the surgery or health centre, or the staff may be able to recommend a chiropodist. Alternatively, you could look in the local telephone directory.

As chiropodists are in rather short supply, it is not usually possible to get attention sufficiently often just to keep toe-nails to a reasonable length. In some areas a nail-cutting service is supplied by a foot care assistant; if you need this, the chiropodist or the local branch of Age Concern should know what is available.

The *Foot Care Book*, available from Age Concern, is useful for reference.

Voluntary bodies
A variety of services are provided by voluntary agencies such as the Red Cross, St John's Ambulance and the WRVS. These may include the loan of home nursing aids such as commodes and bath seats, help with bathing, sitting services, prescription collection, transport to hospital, support for carers and bereavement counselling. Local details can be obtained from the Community Health Council or Age Concern branch.

A variety of self-help organizations exist to help people suffering from a particular disability, or their carers. Their functions vary, but they may produce information books or leaflets, fund practical help measures such as stroke clubs or support groups, and raise money for research. Some of these are listed in the Useful Addresses section at the back of this book, and the doctor, nurse or social worker may tell you of others. You could also consult the *Voluntary Agencies Directory* in the public library.

The Community Health Council
Many people feel at a disadvantage when dealing with health care professionals such as doctors. Still more find it difficult to grasp the intricacies of the system by which health care services are organized. The Community Health Council (CHC) can help to bridge the gap between the providers of health care and its consumers. CHC representatives visit hospitals and clinics to observe services and suggest improvements. They can bring unmet needs to health authorities' attention and give the views of the public on proposed changes like closing hospitals or moving clinics.

Patients find CHCs an invaluable source of information about local health services and how to use them. The secretary and staff can also help with complaints, often through informal contacts, but they can also ensure the best chance of success with a formal complaint by making it through the proper channels in good time.

Community Health Councils often have High Street shop front premises, and are open during office hours. CHC members also meet regularly, and the meetings are open to the public.

Social services

General information on this subject is difficult to provide. There is a good deal of variation around the country in what needs are met and in what way, as well as how often services are provided. Who provides the service, who is deemed eligible for it, and how much is charged also differs from place to place.

Getting a service often requires a certain amount of effort and persistence; frailer clients often become tired and discouraged and give up. Fitter people with good assertiveness and inter-personal skills can help their frailer counterparts both directly, by doing some of the work, and indirectly by insisting on adequate and accessible service provision.

The current aim of local authorities is to provide packages of care to suit individual needs, and the consumer can often put together his or her own package in a similar way, from a variety of sources. One useful approach is to work out beforehand in your own mind what your needs are, as precisely as possible. Then you can try to meet your needs by finding out what is available in your area and how the service works. Your best sources of information are likely to be:

- your local Social Services Department, found in the telephone book under the name of your local authority;
- a Citizens' Advice Bureau, found under 'C' in the telephone book;
- your local Age Concern branch; some produce a booklet describing local services for older people.

In addition, Age Concern England (see page 167) will provide a list of useful fact sheets and other publications on receipt of a stamped addressed envelope.

It is worth cultivating a businesslike approach. Telephone calls are useful for preliminary enquiries, but should be followed up with a letter. It is sensible to file copies of all correspondence and to keep a simple record of telephone calls, with dates, the name of the person spoken to and brief notes of the conversation. All this sounds ponderous, but can save time and trouble in the long run.

Sources of help for some common difficulties are outlined below.

Financial help

Many people take care during their working lives to provide for themselves and their dependants in retirement. Unfortunately, even the most far-seeing and careful of us may find our resources diminished by illness, disability or other unexpected drains on the pocket. It is hardly necessary to point out that state benefits are a right and not charity, and have been earned by many years' hard work.

When the services provided by local statutory and voluntary agencies do not meet your needs, it is often helpful to claim a benefit such as Attendance Allowance and 'buy in' what you require from private sources.

Finding out about statutory benefits

Start by getting in touch with your local branch of the Department of Social Security; you will find the telephone number and address in the telephone book under 'Social Security' or 'Health and Social Security' in older books. Some local authorities employ a welfare rights officer to help applicants get what they are entitled to, and you could ask about this.

The DSS produce a number of leaflets giving details of benefits. You will find these in the DSS office and in some larger post offices, or you can send for them by post from the DSS Leaflets Unit (see page 168). Age Concern's publication *Your Rights* gives details of current benefits and is brought up to date annually.

It is on sale in newsagents and bookshops as well as being available by post from Age Concern.

Grants from voluntary agencies
Voluntary bodies can provide a valuable and flexible source of help, particularly when a single lump sum is required – for instance, for a washing machine to cope with increased laundry due to illness. Many large companies have funds to help retired employees, and there are also associations for particular occupational groups such as musicians and licensed victuallers. Retired service personnel may like to get in touch with the British Legion. A social worker or Citizens' Advice Bureau may be able to advise about likely sources of funds, and a list of organizations can be obtained from the *Annual Charities Register and Digest*, published by the Family Welfare Association; the public library may have a copy.

Help with meals
A variety of services is available for people who have difficulty in cooking for themselves. The best known is Meals on Wheels, when a ready-to-eat meal is delivered by van to the client's home. This may be run by the local Social Services Department or by voluntary agencies such as the WRVS or Age Concern. Kosher foods and diets for other ethnic groups or those with special health needs are sometimes available. While Meals on Wheels are often valuable they have their limitations. There is little or no choice of menu or meal timing. Inevitably there is some delay between cooking and eating, so food becomes less appetizing, with some loss of food value.

Other strategies are being tried in some areas. These include the supply of a small freezer full of oven-ready meals and a microwave oven. This system allows more choice and permits a shorter oven-to-table time, but requires some effort from the client. Once installed it can operate for 365 days a year, whereas the Meals on Wheels service may not be provided over weekends or public holidays.

Luncheon clubs provide a midday meal in some areas. They may be run by Social Services departments, voluntary bodies or by both in partnership. The clubs may be sited in Day Centres where other facilities such as chiropody or hairdressing are conveniently available. While some people enjoy the social contact of a luncheon club others prefer their privacy, and personal taste is important.

It may be that you would much prefer to do your own cooking but are finding this difficult because of a disability. If so, it may help to ask for a visit from the occupational therapist to find out whether new equipment or home adaptations might enable you to use your cooking skills again. The OT can be reached via the Social Services Department. You can also find out about suitable kitchen and home equipment from a Disabled Living Centre; look in Useful Addresses for the Disabled Living Foundation in London and RADAR (Royal Association for Disability and Rehabilitation). Also, if you have not seen the doctor recently you could ask whether there is any new treatment likely to improve your abilities.

Shopping for food can be difficult. In the past the home help (sometimes called a home care worker or domiciliary care worker) has done this, but home helps are now increasingly occupied with personal care tasks. You may be able to find voluntary help through a volunteer bureau, Age Concern branch or church group.

Help with domestic work

A good place to start is with the home help service, run by home help organizers and provided through the Social Services Department. In some places the service now concentrates on personal care to enable very frail people to continue to live at home for as long as possible, and this means that less help is available for housework, etc.

A charge may be made for home help, depending on your income. You may find that private domestic help is more readily available and sometimes even cheaper. Personal recommendation is always useful, and it is wise to take up references before allowing someone into your home. Age Concern England produce a useful fact sheet called *Finding Help at Home*.

Help with personal care

A person who needs help with eating, using the lavatory, keeping clean and moving about is likely to be eligible for Attendance Allowance; you can find out more about this from the DSS office or by obtaining leaflet NI 205 from the DSS Leaflets Unit (see page 168). Someone under sixty-five caring for somebody disabled enough to qualify for Attendance Allowance may be entitled to Invalid Care Allowance; find out more from DSS leaflet NI 212. Both of these benefits can of course be used to 'buy in' suitable care.

In many parts of the country a home care service is provided through the local authority Social Services Department. The helper may be called a home care worker, community care worker or have another similar title. In some areas intensive help is given, with up to five visits to assist with getting up, going to bed, dressing or undressing, eating, toileting and washing. Part of the service may be targeted to people with short-term intensive needs, such as those recently discharged from hospital.

Provision for help with bathing is very variable. In general demand exceeds supply, and an assisted bath can only be offered about once a fortnight. In some places bath aides or nursing auxiliaries visit the client at home; in others the service is supplied at a centre and the client is transported to it. The district nurse or Social Services Department will be able to tell you about bathing services.

Equipment such as a bath seat or a shower might make it possible for you to attend to your needs yourself, and you could ask the Social Services Department for a visit from the occupational therapist. Alternatively you could seek information from the Disabled Living Foundation; among other useful publications is one on *Dressing for the Disabled*.

Making life easier

Help with heating

If the costs of keeping warm in cold weather concern you, it is of course sensible to check that you are claiming all your benefit entitlements. People on Income Support and some other benefits are eligible for extra Cold Weather Payments to cover the extra costs of fuel when the temperature is below freezing. They may also be eligible for grants to pay part of the costs of lagging and draught-proofing their homes; further information can be obtained from the local council or from Age Concern England's fact sheet, *Older Home Owners – financial help with repairs*.

Some people use less heat than they would like to because of anxiety about a large bill for the winter quarter; fuel costs may be easier to meet under a monthly budget scheme. Some people prefer to pay in advance; savings stamps can be bought from gas and electricity showrooms and post offices and used to pay fuel bills. A pre-payment slot metre operated by money tokens or a rechargeable key can sometimes be installed if the appliances to be operated are suitable. Details of pre-payment schemes may vary from place to place, so are best checked with your local gas or electricity showroom.

General advice on the problems of keeping warm can be obtained from the Citizens' Advice Bureau, local Age Concern branch or from the Winter Warmthline on Freephone 0800 289404. A fact sheet, *Help with Heating*, is available from Age Concern England.

Improving communications

Telephones

Some people are entitled to local authority help in getting a telephone and paying for installation costs and rental, though not for calls. People who qualify usually either live alone and may need to call for urgent medical help, or are housebound and rely on the telephone for social contact. Ask the Social Services

Department for more information. Charitable money may also be available; a list of possible sources can be obtained from the *Charities Digest*, possibly available in the public library. It is published by the Family Welfare Association (see page 169).

A forgetful elderly person or someone taken into hospital suddenly may fail to pay a telephone bill and risks being cut off. Such a person can name someone for British Telecom to get in touch with if a bill has not been paid. An application to do this must be countersigned by someone who can confirm the details on the form, such as a district nurse or social worker. For details, see the leaflet *Keeping your Lifeline Open*, available from the BT accounts office address at the top of your telephone bill.

A fact sheet, *Help with Telephones*, is available from Age Concern England.

Alarm systems
Several different types are available. With most, help can be summoned by activating a body-worn trigger device. Some also have wall-mounted buttons or long pull-cords within the reach of someone lying on the floor. Once set off, the alarm puts out an emergency call. Depending on the type, this may automatically dial a friend or relative or alert a special 'Central Control' emergency centre, whose staff can then take appropriate action. Some sorts of alarm allow the user to talk with the person answering the call.

Apart from these types which can be set off in an emergency, there are also passive alarms which send out alarm calls if their buttons are not pushed at regular intervals or if no one moves past a certain point within a given time.

A useful book about alarm systems, *Calling for Help*, is available from Age Concern (see book list). As it is produced by independent agencies, it is a useful supplement to manufacturers' literature. Before investing in an alarm it would be wise to read the book and perhaps to consider the answers to the following questions:

Can the alarm offer more than a telephone alone does? There is no doubt that alarm systems are a boon to some people. It may be reassuring to have a link to a control centre which is staffed twenty-four hours a day, as even the most caring relative cannot always be on the end of a telephone. It may be easier to press a button than make a telephone call if taken suddenly unwell, while someone who falls and is unable to get up can summon help with a body worn trigger when unable to reach a telephone or even an alarm cord.

On the other hand, social contact via an alarm system is usually limited, while regular incoming calls from concerned relatives and friends provides human warmth as well as a check on welfare.

Is the elderly recipient willing to use the alarm? Studies show that trigger devices may be left unworn, alarm cords looped up out of reach and any system left unused in an emergency. Anyone of any age can have an accident, and though the risk of this may become greater as the years pass, many older people do not like to be reminded of this. Indeed, the emphasis on vulnerability may undermine self-esteem and outweigh any imagined benefits of an increased feeling of security.

Can the recipient use the device? A mentally frail person may be unable to learn how to use the new alarm. She will fail to summon necessary help, while triggering frequent false alarms. In addition, some systems pose difficulties for people with disabilities such as deafness, impaired speech and poor dexterity.

How much will it cost? Installation costs, running costs, for example of monitoring by a control centre, maintenance and repairs should all be considered. It is probably better to buy outright rather than rent, except when the alarm will only be needed for a short period such as before a move. Local Authority alarms and monitoring services are cheap; costs vary, and it may be possible to link into a system some distance away, providing the alarm is of a compatible type. Careful 'comparison shopping' is advisable.

Even the best and most appropriate alarm system can only call for assistance and provide limited social contact. As money and services are in short supply, there is a danger of alarm systems being used as cheap substitutes for personal care. This can allow the suppliers of care to feel that 'something has been done' while the real needs of the recipient remain unmet.

Help with getting about

Walking

When walking difficulties come on slowly, medical help may not be sought as with a sudden illness. If pain or stiffness is stopping you getting about and you have not consulted your doctor recently, it may be worth arranging to see him; treatment with drugs and with techniques like joint replacement improve rapidly, and there may be more on offer now than at your last visit.

A physiotherapist can often help an older person to make the best use of faulty joints, for instance by recommending exercises to strengthen wasted muscles. She or he may suggest a walking aid to give you more stability and therefore confidence, and many different types are available.

The familiar walking stick, made from wood or aluminium, can also relieve pain from an arthritic joint by carrying some of its user's weight and thus lightening the load. The stick is usually held in the hand opposite the worst affected side – that is, the *right* hand of someone with a painful left knee: this gives a more natural gait. For maximum weightbearing benefit the stick must be the right length: the measured vertical distance from the top of the handle to the tip should be the same as that from the wrist crease to the ground in a person standing upright, palms forwards. A soft rubber tip or ferrule is important to prevent slipping; ask the suppliers where you can obtain new tips, as these rapidly become worn and unsafe. Handle shape and design may affect your comfort; people with arthritic hands may be helped by padding the handle with foam or felt to a larger, softer shape, and specially moulded handles are sometimes available.

Sticks ending in a pyramid of three or four points (tripods or tetrapods) have a wider base and are more stable. However, they may produce an unnatural walking pattern and are awkward to use on rough ground.

The best-known of the walking frames is the three-sided pulpit-like Zimmer frame. A wheeled frame is more suitable for someone with Parkinson's Disease who has difficulty in starting and stopping walking.

Walking aids are often lent by hospitals or Social Services Departments, but they can also be bought privately. It is often wise to get expert advice from a physiotherapist or occupational therapist on your choice of aid and on how to use it.

Wheelchairs

An outdoor wheelchair pushed by a helper can extend the horizons of someone with poor walking abilities. Another type of chair can be powered by the occupant via the rim on the large rear wheel, and various electrically powered versions are also available.

Wheelchairs can be obtained on free long-term loan through disablement service centres; the application form must be signed by a doctor. Short-term loan – for a disabled visitor, for instance – can be arranged through the Red Cross, other voluntary agency or the Health Authority's medical loans department. Alternatively, chairs can be purchased directly from manufacturers or retailers. Some electrically powered chairs – those used outdoors and controlled by the occupant, for instance – can only be bought privately.

If there is any doubt as to which chair will best meet the needs of its prospective user, it is best to ask for an expert assessment; this may be done at a hospital wheelchair clinic or by an occupational therapist at home. If buying your own, it is probably sensible to make an appointment at a disabled living centre to try out different types. For a list of Disabled

Living Centres around the country, contact RADAR (see page 169).

The 'Orange Badge'

This gives parking concessions to people with restricted mobility, shortening the walking distance to where they want to go. The badge may be used by either the passenger or driver – for instance by the visually handicapped relative of an able-bodied driver, as well as by an amputee who drives an adapted car. Further information can be obtained from Social Services Departments.

Public transport

Able-bodied people There are a variety of concessions for older travellers. Bus companies vary in the size of cost reduction and the age at which a person becomes eligible; in some places off-peak travel may be free, in others half-price, while in a third there may be no concessions at all. Ask the bus company, local authority, Citizens' Advice Bureau or Age Concern branch for local information.

On trains, British Rail give reductions on most services to holders of a Senior Railcard, available to men or women over sixty. A leaflet, 'Senior Railcard', is available at railway stations and includes an application form.

Some concessions are available on long-haul coach rides and for air travel; find out more from the appropriate company or from the travel agent.

A fact sheet, 'Travel Information for Older People', is available from Age Concern England.

Older travellers with a disability The general rules for any sort of travel seem to be to plan well ahead, make special arrangements in good time and to avoid peak time travel whenever possible.

British Rail's leaflet, *British Rail and Disabled Travellers*, available at railway stations, emphasizes the organization's desire to help, and experience confirms that cheerful and kindly assistance is made available whenever possible. However, common sense suggests some limitations: there may be no one available to help a disabled traveller at an unmanned country station, or at a busy suburban one during peak times. If you get in touch by telephone or letter with the staff of your starting station, they should be able to advise about facilities all along your route, and may let you have a booklet describing these for the region. This covers such issues as physical access to booking halls, platforms and lavatories from the street and whether or not there is a 'disabled' toilet or an induction loop system in the booking hall to help the hard of hearing.

Travelling on trains is becoming easier for disabled passengers. Intercity trains have wide doors, grab-rails and spaces in coaches for passengers who cannot transfer to travel in their own wheelchairs. People with limited mobility or needing extra leg-room can reserve a seat without a table near the entrance door and lavatories. On local and suburban routes the new rolling stock has more internal space and wide-access sliding doors whose operating buttons can be reached from a wheelchair. Given notice, station staff will help travellers into their seats, and only those unable to transfer out of their wheelchairs and using older rolling stock should need to travel in the guard's van; BR suggest bringing a companion on such an occasion.

Mobility buses modified to carry wheelchair passengers can be found in some places. In London, Carelink buses run a circular, clockwise service between the London rail termini. The buses have wheelchair lifts, belts and anchorage points for safety and space for luggage and companions. More information can be obtained from London Regional Transport's Unit for Disabled Passengers (see page 169).

People with a visual handicap or with hearing difficulties can also find it difficult to get about. Newly blind people may be helped by the Mobility Officer; find out more from the Social Services Department or the Royal National Institute for the Blind (see page 170). It is worth knowing that guide dogs travel free on trains and are allowed into places like station buffets that usually exclude dogs. Station staff will show visually handicapped passengers to their seats before the barrier is open, so they avoid being jostled in the rush. The RNIB's leaflet, *How to Guide a Blind Person*, is full of information for a visually handicapped person's companion (see book list). Both a disabled person and their companion may be eligible for concessionary fares; ask at the railway station for a leaflet about the Disabled Person's Railcard.

People with a hearing impairment may like to know that many stations have installed induction loop systems in booking halls and also have modified telephones: look for the international symbol of a stylized ear. Of course it is sensible for any hard-of-hearing person to carry a notepad and pencil on journeys, so as to avoid the risk of mishearing important information.

RADAR (Royal Association for Disability and Rehabilitation) is a good source of advice on travel and all other aspects of life with a disability.

Information about Mobility Allowance can be obtained from Social Security Offices (leaflets NI 211 and NI 243).

As health and social service provision is never likely to be generous, it is all the more important to make the best use of what is available. Two things are needed for this: the first is accurate local knowledge and the second, good interpersonal skills. It helps to make personal contacts whenever possible and to find out and use the names of people you come across regularly – the doctor's receptionist, for instance. Being persistent but pleasant in asking for help is not always easy when service providers are rude, offhand or seem deliberately unhelpful. However, it seems to produce the best results in the long run. Finally, never put up with second-rate treatment or services because you are made to feel less deserving than a younger person. Retired people have endured hardships and done work from which the whole community now benefits. In particular they deserve the best from the Welfare State set up by their own efforts. It is high time for society to repay its debt to its older members.

Useful Addresses

When writing to charitable organizations for help, it is advisable to enclose a stamped, self-addressed envelope.

Age Concern England
Astral House
1268 London Road
London SW16 4EJ
Tel: 081–679 8000

Age Concern (Greater London)
54 Knatchbull Road
London SE5
Tel: 071–274 6723

Age Concern (Scotland)
33 Castle Street
Edinburgh EH2 3DN
Tel: 031–225 5000

Alcohol Concern
305 Gray's Inn Road
London WC1X 8QF
Tel: 071–833 3471

Arthritis and Rheumatism
    Council
41 Eagle Street
London WC1R 4AR
Tel: 071–405 8572

ASH (Action on Smoking and
    Health)
5–11 Mortimer Street
London WIN 7RH
Tel: 071–637 9843

BACUP (British Association of
    Cancer United Patients)
121/123 Charterhouse Street
London EC1M 6AA
Tel: 071–608 1661

Breast Care and Mastectomy
    Association
26a Harrison Street
London WC1 8JG
Tel: 071–837 0908

British Association for the Hard
    of Hearing
7–11 Armstrong Road
London W3 7JL
Tel: 081–743 1492

BT Action for Disabled
    Customers
Room B4036, BT Centre

81 Newgate Street
London EC1A 4AJ
Tel: 071–356 4915

Cancer Relief, National Society
   for (Macmillan Fund)
Anchor House
15 Britten Street
London SW3
Tel: 071–351 7811

Carers' National Association
29 Chilworth Mews
London W2 3RG
Tel: 071–724 7776

Chest, Heart and Stroke
   Association
Tavistock House North
Tavistock Square
London WC1H 9JE
Tel: 071–387 3012

Continence Advisers, Association
   of
Disabled Living Foundation
380 Harrow Road
London W9
Tel: 071–289 6111

Colostomy Association, British
38 Eccleston Square
London SW1
Tel: 071–828 5175

Crossroads Care Attendants
   Schemes Ltd, Association of
10 Regent Place
Rugby

Warwickshire CV21 2PN
Tel: 0788–73653

Cruse (Bereavement Care)
Cruse House
126 Sheen Road
Richmond
Surrey TW9 1UR
Tel: 01–940 4818

Diabetic Association, British
10 Queen Anne Street
London W1M 0BD
Tel: 071–323 1531

Disabled Living Foundation
380 Harrow Road
London W9
Tel: 071–289 6111

DSS Leaflets Unit
PO Box 21
Stanmore
Middlesex HA7 1AY

Extend (Exercise Training for the
   Elderly and Disabled)
5 Conway Road
Sheringham
Norfolk NR26 8DD
Tel: 0263–822479/824355

Family Doctor
British Medical Association
BMA House
Tavistock Square
London WC1H 9JR
Tel: 071–387 4499

Family Welfare Association
Central Office
501 Kingsland Road
London E8
Tel: 071–254 6251

Gay Bereavement Project
Unitarian Rooms
Hoop Lane
London NW11 8BS
Tel: 081–455 8894

Greater London Alcohol
    Advisory Service (GLAAS)
91 Charterhouse Street
London EC1
Tel: 071–253 6221

Help the Aged
St James' Walk
London EC1
Tel: 071–253 0253

Hospice Information Service
St Christopher's Hospice
51 Lawrie Park Road
Sydenham
London SE26
Tel: 081–778 9252

Health Education Authority
Hamilton House
Mabledon Place
London WC1H 9TX
Tel: 071–387 9528

Ileostomy Association
Amblehurst House
Black Scotch Lane

Mansfield
Notts NG18 4PF
Tel: 0623 28099

Keep Fit Association
16 Upper Woburn Place
London WC1H 0QG
Tel: 071–387 4349

London Regional Transport Unit
    for Disabled Passengers
55 Broadway
London SW1H 0BD
Tel: 071–222 5600

Marie Curie Memorial Fund
28 Belgrave Square
London SW1X 8QG
Tel: 071–235 3325

Medic-Alert Foundation
17 Bridge Wharf
156 Caledonian Road
London N1 9UU
Tel: 071–833 3034

Parkinson's Disease Society
36 Portland Place
London W1N 3DG
Tel: 071–323 1174

Partially Sighted Society
206 Great Portland Street
London W1
Tel: 071–387 8840

RADAR (Royal Association for
    Disability and Rehabilitation)
25 Mortimer Street

London WIN 8AB
Tel: 071–637 5400

RNIB, Royal National Institute
   for the Blind
224 Great Portland Street
London WIN 6AA
Tel: 071–388 1266

RNID, Royal National Institute
   for the Deaf
105 Gower Street
London WCIE 6AH
Tel: 071–387 8079

Shoe Fitters, Society of
Farley Court
Farley Hill
Reading
Berks RG7 ITT

SPOD (Association to Aid the
   Sexual and Personal
   Relationships of People with a
   Disability)
286 Camden Road

London N7 OBJ
Tel: 071–607 8851

Tinnitus Association, British
105 Gower Street
London WCIE 6AH
Tel: 071–387 8033

University of the Third Age
   (U3A)
c/o 1 Stockwell Green
London SW9 9JF
Tel: 071–737 2541

Widows, National Association of
1st Floor, Neville House
14 Waterloo Street
Birmingham B2 5TX
Tel: 021–643 8348

Women's National Cancer
   Control Campaign
1 South Audley Street
London WI
Tel: 071–499 7532

Book List

When a title has been published by a commercial publisher, you can ask for it from your library or local bookshop. For titles published by national organizations, see the list of addresses on pages 167–70. For free leaflets it is wise to send a large stamped self-addressed envelope or label.

CHAPTER 1: STAYING HEALTHY IN LATER LIFE

Good Eating

Eat Well, Stay Well – Healthy Eating for People over 60 and *Eat Well, Stay Well for Afro-Caribbean Pensioners*. From Age Concern, Greater London, 50p each.

Eating Well on a Budget, BBC Food and Drink Programme and Age Concern, England. From Age Concern, England, £1.50.

Easy Cooking for One or Two by Louise Davies, Penguin Books. From bookshops or libraries.

Sensible Drinking

Alcohol and Elderly People in London. From Age Concern Greater London, 50p.

Alcohol and Older People – Safer Drinking for the Over-60s. From Alcohol Concern or Age Concern, England, free.

That's the Limit! From the Health Education Authority, free.

Smoking

A Smokers' Guide to Giving Up. From the Health Education Authority.

Exercise
The Magic of Movement – a Tonic for Older People by Laura
    Mitchell. From Age Concern, England, £3.95.

Sex, Loving and Relationships
*Living, Loving and Ageing – Sexual and Personal Relationships in
    Later Life* by Wendy Greengross and Sally Greengross. From Age
    Concern, England, £4.95.
Survival Guide for Widows by June Herner and Ann Stanyer. From
    Age Concern, England, £3.50.
Loneliness – How to Overcome It by Val Marriott and Terry
    Timblick. From Age Concern, England, £3.95.

Essential Body Maintenance
The Foot Care Book – an A-Z of Fitter Feet by Judith Kemp. From
    Age Concern, £2.95.

CHAPTER 2: COMMON ILLNESSES

Inexpensive booklets on a range of subjects are available from *Family
Doctor.*

Heart and Blood Vessel Diseases
Living with Angina by Kenneth Gray, 50p.
Heart Disease – 50 questions and the answers.
Reducing the Risk of a Coronary.
Living with a Pacemaker.
These are among a variety of publications from the Chest, Heart and
Stroke Association.

Lungs and Airways
Bronchitis and Emphysema – 20 questions and the answers. From the
    Chest, Heart and Stroke Association.

Nervous System
Stroke – a Handbook for the Patient's Family by Graham Mulley,
    50p.
Home Care for the Stroke Patient in the Early Days by Pamela
    Grasty, 50p.
Learning to Speak Again by Peggy Dalton.

These, among others, are available from the Chest, Heart and Stroke Association.
Parkinson's Disease Patient Information Folder. Among other publications, from the Parkinson's Disease Society.

The Eyes
In Touch with Cataracts by Margaret Ford. From Age Concern, England, £1.
Glaucoma – what you can do about it. From Merck, Sharp and Dohme Ltd, Hoddesdon, Herts. EN11 9BU.

The Ears
Over 60 and Hard of Hearing. Among other publications from British Association for the Hard of Hearing, £5.50.
Hearing Aids – Questions and Answers. Among other publications from the Royal National Institute for the Deaf.

Diabetes
Life with Diabetes by Dr A. Bloom. A *Family Doctor* booklet, £1.20.

Cancer
Understanding Cancer of the Breast.
Understanding Cancer of the Prostate.
Diet and the Cancer Patient.
These are among other publications from BACUP's Cancer Information Service.

CHAPTER 3: YOUR MEDICINES

Know your Medicines by Pat Blair. From Age Concern, £3.95.
Principal Drugs by S. J. Hopkins, Faber and Faber. From bookshops.

CHAPTER 4: GETTING HELP

A variety of free fact sheets are available from Age Concern, England. These provide up-to-date and impartial advice on subjects such as help with writing, travel concessions, etc.

Patients' Rights – a summary of your rights and responsibilities in the NHS. From Community Health Councils, free.

You and Your Dentist by National Consumer Council. HMSO, £2.50.

Your Rights by Sally West. From Age Concern, England, £1.50.

Your Taxes and Savings by John Burke and Sally West. From Age Concern, England, £2.70.

Heating Help in Retirement, Energy Inform Ltd. From Age Concern, England, £1.

British Telecom's Guide to Equipment and Services for Disabled Customers. From your local BT Sales Office, or from BT Action for Disabled Customers.

Calling for Help – a Guide to Emergency Alarm Systems. From Age Concern, England, £2.95.

How to Guide a Blind Person. From the RNIB, free.

If Only I'd Known that a Year Ago – a guide for newly disabled people, their families and friends. From RADAR. Single copies free with a stamped self-addressed envelope.

Index

Main references are in bold type.

doctor, family, *see* general
practitioner
dopamine, 59, *120*
drinking, and fluid intake, 7–8
see also alcohol
driving, health and safety aspects,
16–17, 19, 60, 104
drugs, *see* medicines
DSS Leaflets Unit, *155*, 168

ears, 69–72
eating, healthy, 4–7
enjoyment of, 7, 9–10
ECG (electrocardiogram), 39, 40
ECT (electroconvulsive therapy),
62
elastic stockings, 43
electricity, safety precautions,
21–2
emergency calls to doctors, 144–
5
emphysema, 12
enemas, 117
evening classes, 29
exercise, *5*, 13–15, 28, 40, 74
Extend (Exercise Training for the
Elderly and Disabled), 14,
168
eyes, 31, 36, *63–9*
treatment for diseases of, 124–
5, 132
shingles, 63
see also diabetes; Partially
Sighted Society; RNIB;
visual handicap

fainting, 39
Fallopian tubes, 53

falls, 13, 14, *19–21*, 35, 74
and heart problems, 39, 40
Family Health Services Authority
(formerly Family Practitioner
Committee), 141–3, 146,
151, 152
Family Welfare Association, *156*,
160, 169
fat
on body, and change in shape,
4–5
in diet, 8–9
fibre, dietary, *7*, 31, 46–7, 49,
52
fires, safety precautions, 21–2
'flu, 44–5
food, 4–10
foot care, *32–3*
arterial disease and, 42
diabetes and, 84, 86
fractures, 9, *74–5*
'frozen shoulder', 79–80
fruit and vegetables, *8*, 51

gall bladder disease, 52
gallstones, 52
treatment of, 116
gangrene, 41, 42
gastroscopy, 48
Gay Bereavement Project, *26*, 30,
169
general practitioner, *139–45*,
146–7
genitals, 53–5
treatment for diseases of, 118–
19
geriatric liaison nurse, 148
geriatric units, 38
geriatrician, 38